June Sarpong OBE is one of the most recognizable British television presenters and broadcasters and a prominent activist, having co-founded the WIE Network (Women: Inspiration and Enterprise) and the Decide Act Now summit. In 2019, she was appointed the first ever Director of Creative Diversity at the BBC.

June is the author of *Diversify,* an empowering guide to why a more open society means a more successful one, and *The Power of Women,* which proves the importance of feminism in the personal, social, and economic progress of society as a whole.

The Power of Privilege

How white people can challenge racism

June Sarpong

ONE PLACE. MANY STORIES

HQ
An imprint of HarperCollins*Publishers* Ltd
1 London Bridge Street
London SE1 9GF

This edition 2020

1

First published in Great Britain by
HQ, an imprint of HarperCollins*Publishers* Ltd 2020

A catalogue record for this book is
available from the British Library.

ISBN: 978-0-00-843592-9

Typeset in Bembo by
Palimpsest Book Production Ltd, Falkirk, Stirlingshire

Printed and bound in Great Britain by
CPI Group (UK) Ltd, Croydon, CR0 44Y

For more information visit: www.harpercollins.co.uk/green

To anyone who has the
desire and drive to do better.

CONTENTS

Dear Reader,

Recent events around racial injustice have inspired many with agency and privilege in society to ask, 'what can I do?' and 'how can I be an effective ally?' We are way beyond the point of empty rhetoric – our actions must embody our ideals. Equality must be designed by each and every one of us. The challenge may be great, but it is certainly not insurmountable, and we all have a part to play.

This book will help to identify the capacity that you, the reader, has to build the fair and just society that the better part of ourselves knows to be possible. I'd like to personally thank you for embarking on this important journey of positive change with me. There will be some uncomfortable moments, but getting comfortable with being uncomfortable is a major first step in making a real difference.

THE POLARIZED PRESENT

The white man's happiness cannot be purchased by the black man's misery.

Frederick Douglass

Racism
Racism is the belief that people of some races are inferior to others, and the behaviour which is the result of this belief. Racism also refers to the aspects of a society which prevent people of some racial groups from having the same privileges and opportunities as people from other races.
Collins English Dictionary

Anti-racism
Anti-racism is an active and conscious effort to work against multidimensional aspects of racism.
Robert J. Patterson

Other (noun)
A person of a marginalized or excluded group or demographic within society.

Otherize or otherizing (verb)
To exclude or facilitate the exclusion of an individual or group through action or inaction.

Otherism (noun)
A conscious or unconscious bias that is formed through ignorance or conditioning that results in beliefs or actions that exclude individuals or groups deemed different or 'other'.

Otherizing happens when our brains make incredibly quick judgments and assessments of people and situations, often without us realizing. Our prejudices are influenced by our background, culture and personal experiences. Without us actively exploring and challenging our limiting beliefs we can be inadvertently complicit in fuelling inequality.
Diversify.org

★

As a child growing up on a council estate in London's East End, I can remember my Ghanaian immigrant parents drumming into me the idea that I was going to need to 'work twice as hard for half as much'. I don't remember ever asking them, 'Work twice as hard for half as much as who?' And they never explicitly stated who the 'who' was. They didn't need to – the signs were everywhere. From my young, impressionable eyes, I could see for myself that everything that represented power and privilege was white – primarily white and male . . . and the opposite of me.

This is a conversation that every child of colour raised in the West will have had with their parents or caregivers. They might not recall when they first had '*the conversation*', but they will remember having had it. For non-white children growing up as minorities in Europe or North America, the first uncomfortable conversation with parents isn't about the birds and the bees – that comes later. Much more pressing matters come first: the harsh realities of the discrimination that is likely to impact them the moment they leave the safety of their parents' home and enter the world. White children have the luxury of waiting until their tweens before having to learn about the realities of life. Sadly, children of colour are told much earlier, and their conversation is about the inequities they will invariably face at some point, no matter how talented or brilliant they might be.

I describe in the foreword of the British edition of *Black Enough*, Ibi Zoboi's book of short stories for teens, that this is a heartbreaking burden that parents of colour or white parents of non-white children have to bear. Children of mixed-race heritage are one of the fastest-growing ethnic groups in Britain, and this is a rapidly increasing trend in the USA too, so now many parents who might not themselves have a lived experience of discrimination are having to have the '*the conversation*'.

'*The conversation*' meant I didn't complain when my parents berated me for my less than A★ report card, or for my tardiness, or corrected my grammar, spelling or mispronunciations – even though they had heavy African accents themselves, they demanded their children speak the 'Queen's English' – because the stakes were higher for me. I wasn't on a level playing field. No, it wasn't fair, but it was the reality, and I had to make the most of the hand I'd been dealt. My parents' journey to the UK had not been an easy one, so in comparison to all they had experienced, my dose of inequality did not seem worthy of complaint. There were no excuses – no matter what, they still expected the best from me and my siblings. The only problem was that inequality meant second-generation immigrant kids like me might not actually be given the opportunity to be able to do our best.

My first book, *Diversify*, examined the social, moral and economic benefits of diversity and explained why inclusive societies are better for everyone. While promoting *Diversify*, I found myself travelling all over the world having conversations around the sorts of prickly subjects we are supposed to avoid in polite company, subjects such as gender, class, sexual orientation, race and religion. I mediated while those from both underrepresented and privileged groups engaged in difficult yet brutally honest and open dialogue. I listened while people bravely voiced their concerns, hurts, frustrations, confusion, shame and guilt. I was heartened and humbled by the sorts of breakthroughs I saw take place between, friends, families, colleagues and strangers. The kind of understanding I witnessed made me more hopeful than ever, even in such divisive times. However, even with these breakthroughs, wherever I went there was an ever-present elephant in the room, the role of the main beneficiaries of our unfair system: white people, particularly privileged white men.

The concept of privilege

The concept of privilege can be a challenging one to get across, but it's one of the key factors that has shaped the inequalities, imbalances, and prejudices of society today. In order to fix the problem, the first step is acknowledging it.
Nicholas Conley

The term 'white privilege' has become part of the common lexicon, but what does it actually mean, how does it play out in real life and how can you become aware of it if you are one of its beneficiaries? In her famed 1989 essay 'White Privilege: Unpacking the Invisible Knapsack', American scholar and antiracism activist Peggy McIntosh brilliantly describes her breakthrough in fully understanding this concept and all that it affords her:

I think whites are carefully taught not to recognize white privilege, as males are taught not to recognize male privilege. So I have begun in an untutored way to ask what it is like to have white privilege. I have come to see white privilege as an invisible package of unearned assets which I can count on cashing in each day, but about which I was 'meant' to remain oblivious.[1]

It's so important that those afforded privilege no longer remain 'oblivious'. This is not about shame or guilt, and certainly not superiority or pity either. It is about understanding this elevated position and exploring the concept of privilege and the systemic benefits universally accrued to members of the majority group. The late US academic Allan G. Johnson spent much of his working life explaining and challenging this concept. In a blog post titled 'What is a system of privilege?' Johnson describes privilege as being organized around three principles: dominance, identification, and centredness.

For example, a system of white privilege, through being 'white-dominated', results in white people almost always occupying societal positions of power – a person of colour inhabiting this position is consequently seen to be an exception. White-dominance, Johnson explains, can be seen in Barack Obama being described as the black President, and not just 'the President'.

This white-dominated society further leads to 'white-identification', through which white people begin to be identified as the norm. Everyone who falls outside of this category (often people of colour) are defined by what they are not, 'non-white', rather than what they are. It would be strange for one group of people to be set as the standard for all humans without there being a reason for it, and so society constructs the most logical explanation: that white people are the norm because they are to be seen as superior. As Johnson goes on to explain:

Several things follow from this, including seeing the way they do things as simply 'human' or 'normal,' and giving more credibility to their views than to the views of 'others', in this case people of color. White-identification also encourages whites to be unaware of themselves as white, as if they didn't have a race at all. It also encourages whites to be unaware of white privilege.[2]

These two principles, combined with 'white-centredness' (putting white people in the centre of attention, from newspapers and books to films and TV) result in white people being afforded unprecedented amounts of opportunity and advantage simply because they are white.

How to reimagine a future where the rest of society is afforded the same access to the opportunity that has been the private domain of privileged white men for so long is a question that has long perplexed those of us on the inclusion mission, along with how to honestly call out inequality without demonizing the very group that has the tightest grip on the levers of prosperity. The data is clear: white men account for 72 per cent of corporate leadership in Fortune 500 companies surveyed, and in the UK there are only six female heads of FTSE 100 companies.[3,4] So, if more equality in the workplace, and beyond, is the goal, then white men need to be involved. But what can the group who have the most agency in society do to effect long-lasting, positive change? What can the group whose ancestors created the current imbalance we live under do to help create a new, more inclusive normal and perhaps help correct some of the wrongs of the past? In this book I aim to answer these questions as best I can, as well as offering ten concrete actions that people of privilege can undertake to make things better.

Though I have so far mainly mentioned privileged white men, there is also an incredibly important role for allies across the board, particularly white women. Amongst the groups representing those of diverse characteristics, white women from affluent backgrounds undoubtedly are those with the most agency in society and are likely to have the closest proximity to their male equivalents who are in the most privileged group. This enables white women of privilege to be powerful allies for any of the other groups. Because of the sheer number of those impacted, gender equality, as an inclusion discussion, is usually be led by white women. But there is an easy opportunity here to display inclusion by highlighting intersectional aspects of gender, such as race, and sharing platforms with other groups of women marginalized by additional characteristics of exclusion.

Having an understanding of discrimination based on gender, white women have an opportunity to empathize and build coalitions between a range of diverse groups, using their position in the power structure to build bridges.

It is also important to note that as we strive towards gender parity, I do not assume that all white men have privilege – not for one second. Of course, race and sex are physical characteristics that can easily be recognized on sight and used to positively or negatively classify an individual depending on how similar or different they are from the 'norm'. However, even individuals who have the elevated characteristics of being male and white may also be denied the level of agency that often flows from that association. Obviously, the lived experience of working-class or low-income white males greatly differs from that of elite or privileged white men, as does the experience of white women of differing socioeconomic backgrounds.

This is something we have witnessed in recent years with the rise of forgotten white working-class males who are not succeeding in state schools and who as a result of globalization are losing their traditional manual and semi-skilled occupations. This, ironically, is due more often than not to more affluent, more educated white men outsourcing jobs abroad and creating innovations in technology that undermine traditional working-class jobs. These economic shifts have placed the white males who rely on manual work at a disadvantage to educated non-whites and women, who are more able to attain or develop the skills needed for well-paid, highly skilled jobs. A degree of resentment has therefore understandably arisen from less-privileged white men whose issues have been ignored because they are lumped in with white male privilege at large.

Another group of white males whose elevated characteristics do not insulate them from discrimination are those with (L)GBTQ+ identities. They might not be 'out' or visibly or audibly different from other elite white males, so they may avoid some elements of prejudice. However, at some point in their lives – perhaps when they begin to recognize their true identities – many will experience alienation from a society that was not designed with them in mind. The added burden of knowing that you are perceived by some (30 per cent in the USA and 20 per cent in the UK) as a moral problem and that strangers have opinions about what you should be allowed to do with your life is an extra layer of baggage that gay men must contend with, irrespective of how well off they are. Societal rejection is also something that white males with a disability experience, albeit of a different kind to that of gay men. In this case, moral outrage is instead replaced with pity, misunderstanding and gross underestimation.

With all of that said, and allowing for instances of intersectionality, there is no getting away from the fact that if you are a white, non-disabled, educated, heterosexual, middle-aged, middle- or upper-class male adhering to a version of Christianity or atheism that fits within the confines of a secular liberal democracy, then you are part of a minority that is not deemed as 'other' on some level by Western society, sparing you from the most obvious levels of discrimination.

From accusation to conversation

When it comes to inclusion, of course everyone must play their part in creating the change we seek. However, those with the most power can have the maximum impact, whether that be positively or negatively. This book aims to help assist those with the most privilege to become effective allies – those perched at the top of the hierarchy of inclusion and fortunate enough not to be 'otherized' by mainstream Western society, who not only want to understand their privilege but also to use that privilege for good.

The circulation across social and traditional media of the video of the horrific and inhumane killing of George Floyd, an unarmed black man, at the hands of police officers in the USA in 2020 has meant that people across the world have been exposed to the brutality of racism.[5] Opinions about the wider severity of racism will usually depend on proximity and exposure. Generally, white people in majority-white countries will have had limited exposure to racism, whereas black people, especially from lower socioeconomic groups, will have had direct experience of it and will therefore have a more pronounced view of its severity and prevalence. However, witnessing the same incident through the same mobile-phone lens meant that the racism experienced by black Americans suddenly became a visual reality for white people. There was no escaping it, no justification or narrative to present the killing as accidental or in some way caused by the action of the victim.

The full implications of white privilege were cemented by the George Floyd murder and video coming just twenty-four hours after the circulation of another video. This video depicted Amy Cooper, a white woman, threatening to call the police on Christian Cooper (no relation), a black birdwatcher in Central Park in New York, after he had asked her to put a leash on her dog, which was running free in an area of the park where that was prohibited. As she became increasingly annoyed at his request and the fact that he was videoing her response, she proceeded to call the police, intimating to them that a black man was threatening her.[6] This was the latest in a long line of white women weaponizing their fear of black men, leading all the way back to fourteen-year-old Emmett Till in 1955, who was lynched after being accused of whistling at Carolyn Bryant.

As the killing of Floyd the day after the Cooper incident demonstrated, interactions between the police and black people in America are fraught with danger. Floyd did not resist arrest, instead doing everything he would have been taught to minimize his chances of being hurt, but he still ended up dead. And this is the reality for many black people, and why the issue goes much deeper than a few bad apples. If you are black, a white person has the power to threaten your very existence.

As outrage followed the global circulation of the footage, the subsequent demonstrations and civil disturbances have forced a very public conversation about race in which white people have had to play an active part. Normally these conversations are reserved for cultural celebrations, such as Black History Month, with white people taking a more passive role. However, there is now an acknowledgement, especially amongst younger generations, that racism is pervasive and the responsibility to address it lies with majority white populations. It is no longer just a marginal, unseen issue for people of colour. The footage of both events coming so close together left no room for ambiguity about the reality of racism – and it became clear that it is a problem for white people too.

Admittedly, when we talk about ways to increase diversity, we don't immediately think of straight white males, as they are often viewed as the source of the problem more than part of the solution, with tags like 'pale, male and stale' being used to describe them. Yes, much of the inequality we see globally has been the design of a small, elite group of mainly straight white men, whether that be in Western society or former colonies. However, a shared identity doesn't have to mean identical views or collective guilt but rather an opportunity to join a conversation. One of the main stumbling blocks on the journey towards greater inclusion has been the inability to effectively engage those who are currently the most catered for in society in a discussion around inclusion and widening participation.

There is no getting away from the truth that white males currently control the bulk of the world's capital and resources, and, yes, some of the most affluent members of this group have used their power to marginalize or exploit those whom they have deemed as 'other', today and in the past. However, there is also no getting away from the fact that if we want this power and agency to be shared more widely and equitably without conflict or casualties then a productive dialogue needs to take place, preferably with the focus on honesty and acceptance rather than guilt and blame.

Having spent the best part of the last four years researching, writing and then speaking about the benefits of diversity for society, one question that has kept coming up from white people, often men, in audiences, offices and boardrooms I have visited is 'I know I am seen as the main cause of the problem, but what can I do?'

I'd been toying with the idea for some time of writing about privileged people who want to create change and an incident at a diversity dinner I hosted made me realize there was a need for a book such as this – the recent fallout from the senseless killing of George Floyd only made that need all the more urgent. I'd been asked by a major consulting firm to lead an unconscious-bias training dinner for some of their senior employees and high-level clients. At my table, there was a young, white professional couple whom I really bonded with. I was waxing lyrical about why I believed in the importance of workplace targets and goals as the quickest means of levelling the playing field. Having been in television for more than two decades, I have become very adept at sensing energy and reading people. As I continued talking about race, class and gender, I could sense the husband's discomfort at some of what I was saying. This wasn't necessarily a problem; the whole point of the dinner was for us to move outside of our comfort zones.

However, I wanted to make sure I understood his viewpoint in order to figure out a way to include him and people like him in my conversations around equality. So I asked him for his honest opinion. What he said struck me and has stayed with me throughout the process of writing this book. Even with his discomfort, he was still eager to know how he could be of help in creating change. He also wanted to understand if there was indeed a place for him in the conversation: 'How do we move from accusation to conversation and that I not to be made to feel like I'm on trial just because I happen to be white and male?' To that I added 'and middle class', at which he was quick to point out to me that he was not 'middle class', even though many people assumed he was because of his current privileged status. He had worked hard and won scholarships to rise through the ranks of a world that saw him as an insider, even though the reverse was true. That evening was a powerful moment of revelation for me and all those who were in attendance, and confirmed that there was a need for someone to write in a balanced, meaningful way about what white people in positions of power and privilege can do to bring about positive change.

We are all essentially informed by our beliefs, which are the summary of the stories we tell ourselves. The prevailing story that we are all told in the West is one of hard-fought battles for equality and an arc towards justice and greater meritocracy – not a perfect arc but one that is improving. The experiences of people of colour, especially those who are socially disadvantaged, meant that this story was long ago discarded as a fable. Others who have made some progress in a white world buy in to the story but see it as aspirational rather than literal and are careful not to challenge it in an attempt to avoid the potential cost of rocking the boat. However, the naked brutality of the treatment of black people, in America and around the world, has caused people of colour to break their silence, tired of playing along with the official story. Many white people also feel outraged and have found themselves marching alongside people of colour, demanding that a fair and meritocratic society be delivered. But those mainly white people who have excelled under the current system also have to come to terms with the reality that they are the ones who have prospered from systemic racism.

One of the key measures of agency in our society is wealth, and it is another indicator that singles out the black community. The underrepresentation of black people in elite professions and their absence from wealth listings is contrasted with an overrepresentation in the lower socioeconomic stratas of society. Economic empowerment will be a key milestone in enabling black people to resist racism, as opposed to needing to be defended from it. Owning businesses, being the employer rather than the employee and having the options that wealth provides can help to mitigate black people's exposure to racism. However, economic empowerment is taking longer to achieve than many of us hoped it would.

In 2019, I was contacted by Eleanor Mills, the then Editor of the *Sunday Times Magazine*, to write a piece about the blatant lack of diversity in the Rich List. There's a famous quote by the American campaigner for children's rights Marian Wright Edelman that says: 'You can't be what you can't see'. Well, I was shocked to see just one black female entrepreneur represented. I am speaking specifically of black women here rather than women of colour, as there was a stark contrast in the Rich List between the number of Asian entrepreneurs (more than 80) and the number of black entrepreneurs (four, three of whom were men).[7] The following year nothing had changed, and Shingi Mararike had to write a piece not too dissimilar to the one I had written the year before. This must change if we are to make any progress towards equality.

Patriarchal rules

In Europe, elite white men have been at the top of the totem pole for centuries. The descendents of the brutally successful male warlords who initially established themselves as the ruling elites in Europe were able to take their brand of patriarchy and make it global. This was achieved by the creation of a formidable coalition of ambitious maritime 'explorers', the Christian church and a heavily biased education system. As European men began to dominate the planet militarily, politically and culturally from the sixteenth century onwards, the propagation of the idea that being born straight, white, male and Christian made you superior to those who lacked even one of these characteristics became incredibly powerful.

This idea grew to such prominence that those who were born with these elevated characteristics came to see it as not only their right but their moral duty to dominate those inferiors who happened to be lacking these characteristics. If you were absent any one of them, you needed to be controlled, protected, civilized or suppressed, or you were a moral abomination. Even though not all straight white males benefited equally, this idea resonated and led to a feeling of pride in those who did share all of the elevated characteristics and an assumption of superiority. The idea that a person was innately better than those individuals who lacked any of these characteristics became commonplace around the world. In fact, the belief in these elevated characteristics became so prominent that it led to education, opportunity and achievement becoming intrinsically linked to the elite group who held these characteristics.

This elite group have obtained the bulk of the world's wealth and have created a framework that allows them to be the most likely to fulfil their potential in society. If truth be told, the origins of a lot of this wealth has been ill-gotten, to the detriment of much of what we now consider to be the developing world. This historical context has created an entrenched position of privilege, leading to the systemic racism we continue to see today, making it very difficult to challenge without buy-in from the people at the top of the hierarchy.

The case for why

Beyond simple fairness, there are very practical reasons why we need to create the conditions where inclusion and diversity are the norm. In the UK, the Social Mobility Commission enlisted Ipsos MORI to conduct a poll in February 2016 on intergenerational social mobility. The results indicated that the majority of Britons felt the country's best days were behind it: 54 per cent believed that young people's lives would be worse than those of previous generations, and even more worryingly only one in five believed that better days lay ahead. These findings should have been a warning about the growing dissatisfaction of hardworking everyday Brits.

Alan Milburn, Chair of the Social Mobility Commission from 2012 to 2017, is convinced that these concerns are real and very valid and should have been heeded. He told me:

> Britain's deep social mobility problem, for this generation of young people in particular, is getting worse, not better. The barriers to progress are becoming bigger, not smaller. The impact is no longer only felt by the poorest in our society but instead is holding back a whole tranche of low- and middle-income families . . .
>
> Whole tracts of Britain feel left behind. Whole communities feel the benefits of globalization have passed them by. Whole sections of society feel they are not getting a fair chance to succeed.

Famed thinker Noam Chomsky explains how the same thing has happened in the USA. In his film and book *Requiem for the American Dream*, he draws on the history of US economic inequality to show the crucial difference between then and now:

> During the Great Depression, things were much worse than they are today, but there was an expectation that things were going to get better. There was a real sense of hopefulness. There isn't today . . .

Not only is it extremely unjust in itself, inequality has highly negative consequences on the society as a whole because the very fact of inequality has a corrosive, harmful effect on democracy.[8]

There has always been inequality, but today the disparity between rich and poor has created a global wealth divide. According to a pre-World Economic Forum 2017 report by Oxfam, eight billionaires control as much wealth as the poorest 50 per cent of the world.[9] The unfair consequences of globalization have created a new class, described by economist Guy Standing in his book *The Precariat: The New Dangerous Class*. Standing explains that the new 'precariat' has 'precarious living standards characterized by low income in insecure employment'.[10] But this level of inequality is unsustainable – the people who have been left behind, very many of whom are people of colour, will only tolerate this for so long. Therefore, it is only by creating a more conscious and inclusive form of capitalism that we can hope to avoid widespread unrest in the future.

There's also a very lucrative and sizeable upside to being more inclusive. A 2015 report by McKinsey showed that the more diverse the company, especially at the leadership level, the more profitable it was. Perhaps even more importantly, diverse teams have been proven to be smarter and more effective than homogenous ones: they have a tendency to focus more on facts; are more objective; process data more carefully; and are more innovative.[11]

And just as the ideas and contributions of a diverse and inclusive group lead to better outcomes in business, the same is true in life more generally. This is why it is for the benefit of everyone that we do all we can to avoid the dangers of growing inequality and embrace everything that diversity has to offer.

How this book works

This book looks at some of the ways in which race inequality manifests itself, before demonstrating how to be an effective ally in a world that is evolving at a rapid pace, how to use the power of privilege for good and how to create a bigger, more inclusive pie that provides more slices to go around. This involves thinking about the kind of legacy you as an individual wish to leave behind and not blindly enjoying the benefits of a system that is causing so much waste of human potential. Business as usual is not working and cannot safely take us any further in our human journey.

The COVID-19 pandemic has exposed the tragic extent of racial inequality in the West, with people of colour dying disproportionately. Although further research will be needed to fully understand why this is the case, it is thought that living in densely populated, poor urban areas, often within tightly situated apartment blocks and often in multigenerational households, has left many people of colour highly vulnerable to the destructive nature of this deadly virus. These are often the same people in frontline jobs ensuring that we are able to access groceries, use public transport and of course receive medical care. And BAME (black, Asian and minority ethnic) people are more likely to suffer from pre-existing conditions as a result of health inequalities.[12] These deaths have exposed horrible racial inequities and are especially tragic when they occur amongst those who have sacrificed their own lives working to save the lives of their fellow human beings. The very least we owe to those extraordinary individuals is to finally address systemic racism. The inequalities exposed by the virus are more visible now, so we can see exactly where they occur, whether it be in housing, health, education or employment. This provides the perfect opportunity to marshal resources where they are needed to directly address racial disparities. Just as with the depth of racism that has been exposed by George Floyd's tragic death, to remain ignorant is now inexcusable. We can instead choose to opt for a different reality, where we do what is needed to ensure we can all live with human dignity and enjoy the same life chances regardless of the colour of our skin.

The Power of Privilege outlines ten action-driven solutions to create the right kind of change, by equipping those with elevated characteristics to harness their privilege and agency, and become effective allies for inclusion.

We know the usual way of doing things is not working; the patience of people on the receiving end of discrimination is also wearing thin. The old ideas that there are people who are inferior and can be treated less favourably at work or by the state for lacking an elevated characteristic is being challenged at large. But we need a few more good people to use their privilege in support of those with less power, not simply as an act of charity but rather as a display of allyship and solidarity. When someone is not heard or marginalized as a result of their identity, it demonstrates the failure of our systems. Those people then begin to disengage and their participation in the system is lost.

Now more than ever it is imperative that everyone is 'in the room' as we navigate social, economic and demographic changes in the West alongside environmental and geopolitical shifts globally. This book seeks to separate the bystanders from the leaders who are prepared to subvert the normal patterns that reinforce the supremacy of white people to achieve a different and more inclusive outcome. If you are a white person who wants to add being 'inclusive' as a legitimate elevated characteristic to your identity, then here is where you learn about the real power of privilege.

OUR PAINFUL PAST

Who controls the past controls the future. Who controls the present controls the past.

George Orwell, *1984*

A black child growing up in America or Europe will, by the time he reaches school, already have an understanding that he is different from the majority. Whether it's the images she sees in the media, or family members attempting to prepare her for the exclusion she's likely to experience outside the home, she will know that the rules are not the same for her and children that look like her. In many cases, he will be told, as I was, that anything is possible, but that he has to be twice as good and work twice as hard as his white counterparts in order to succeed and be worthy of acceptance. Many will take this message on board and strive for academic excellence in a pressured education system. Others, seeing black role models in sport, music, cinema or some other art form, will pursue a career in those fields, hoping that their talent (as has been the case with stars such as Jay-Z and Beyoncé, Usain Bolt, Serena Williams, LeBron James, Zoe Saldana, Will Smith, Lizzo, Stormzy, and Tinie Tempah) will enable them to overcome discrimination and other obstacles to success.

My family experienced this first-hand. My father was gifted and well educated as a child and rose to become somebody of stature in his native Ghana, but when he arrived in Britain as an immigrant in the 1980s he had to start afresh. A political coup in Ghana meant that he had lost his position and his finances. He still had his education and experience, though, which surely would be enough for him to make a new life for himself and his family? Unfortunately not. In 1980s Britain, his thick foreign accent and skin colour meant he was visibly and audibly different from the sort of person employers assumed was suitable for a job in banking. There was an unwritten understanding that non-white migrants from Commonwealth countries could settle in the UK to do menial or low-paid jobs that indigenous people didn't want to do. Immigrants like my father, regardless of education and career experience, were not going to be allowed to just parachute into middle-class occupations like banking.

It soon became clear to my father that Britain was not going to be the land of opportunity he had first hoped, so he decided to take his talents and my brother to America. America did provide more opportunities, and Dad was able to secure a job in banking and then eventually launch his own successful real-estate and construction company. Perhaps America, despite its poorer record on race relations, was more amenable than the UK to the idea of social mobility for an African man.

Starting again for the second time in America was not easy, but Sam Sarpong Sr thrived against insurmountable odds and built a very comfortable upper-middle-class life, and I can't help but beam with pride when I look at the journey he has made. A few years ago, I made a pilgrimage to the rural village he was raised in, and I couldn't fully comprehend the vast leap from where my father started in life to where he now resides. I doubt I would have had the same level of grit and determination to overcome such odds.

Life wasn't all smooth sailing for my brother, Sam Sarpong Jr, either. African in parentage, British by birth and raised in America – as you can imagine, he didn't fit neatly into any particular category. As an actor–entertainer, my brother harboured a desire for visible signs of affluence – luxury cars, designer clothes and beautiful women. However, as flamboyant as he was, during one of my visits to America I saw my brother become humble pretty fast. Driving through Los Angeles in one such luxury car, Sam was pulled over by the police. This being a regular occurrence for black people, but particularly black men in America, Sam had his contrite responses memorized: 'Yes sir, no sir, sorry officer', etc.

Witnessing this exchange and knowing the type of person Sam was, I felt upset and indignant – especially as he had done nothing wrong and there appeared to be no valid reason for the stop. My friend and mentor Baroness Margaret McDonagh – white and well spoken – was also with us in the car. As Sam delivered his usual routine, Margaret and I weren't so agreeable, as this is not something either of us were accustomed to. We demanded the officer's badge number and a detailed explanation as to why we were stopped. The police officer seemed taken aback, as he hadn't expected to be met by two British women, and his tone changed immediately to become less threatening and more like a public servant. We received the badge number but no valid reason for why we were pulled over.

With US police officers being fully armed, black men in the USA have to humble themselves to an almost humiliating degree to ensure their survival each time they encounter law enforcement, and sometimes not even that is enough, as was the case with Eric Garner, Michael Brown, Tamir Rice, Breonna Taylor, George Floyd, Rayshard Brooks and many others.[13] Regardless of the outcome of these exchanges, they serve as an overt reminder to all young black people that, whatever your achievements, aspirations or character, you can be brought down to the level of a criminal at any time. Male pride makes this a difficult reality to live with and can generate anger in the most excluded and vulnerable black men. However, anger and resentment at authority are costly emotions that black men can ill afford in Western society. In both the UK and the USA, it's an uncomfortable truth that in spite of claims of equality and calls for fair treatment, young black men in particular continue to be targeted for no other reason than the colour of their skin.

These stories show just how difficult it is for black people – even those of education and affluence – to negotiate life in the UK and USA as an 'other'. Their colour is always the first thing people see. But where did this obsession with race and skin colour come from? And why have we allowed it to become such a divisive and alienating factor in our society? These are fundamental questions that scientists may now be able to answer for us. And perhaps, by answering them, we can tear them down.

The false social construct of race

Race is the child of racism, not the father.
Ta-Nehisi Coates, *Between the World and Me*

Anthropologist Nina Jablonski has conducted extensive studies into this issue from her research lab at Pennsylvania State University. I've been lucky enough to spend time with Jablonski and listen to her speak about the origins of the social construct of race – her findings are fascinating. In her book *Living Color: The Biological and Social Meaning of Skin Color*, Jablonski investigates 'the social history of skin color from prehistory to the present' and finds that, biologically, 'race' simply does not exist.[14] In a separate article, she states, 'Despite ever more genetic evidence confirming the nonexistence of races, beliefs in the inherent superiority and inferiority of people remain part of the modern world'.[15] And she goes on to explain that the most influential ideas on the formation of historic racism came from just one man:

> The philosopher Immanuel Kant (1724–1804) was the first person to classify people into fixed races according to skin color. To him and his followers, skin color was equated with character. People of darker-colored races were inferior and destined to serve those of lighter-colored races. Kant's ideas about color, race, and character achieved wide and lasting acceptance because his writings were widely circulated, his reputation good, and his audience naïve. The 'color meme' was born. The linking of blackness with otherness and inferiority was one of the most powerful and destructive intellectual constructs of all time. Views on the inherent superiority and inferiority of races were readily embraced by the intelligentsia of Western Europe and eventually by the general populace because they supported existing stereotypes.[16]

It's hard to overstate the damage this kind of thinking has done over the centuries. Geneticist Spencer Wells, founder of The Genographic Project and author of *The Journey of Man*, goes even deeper, using the science of DNA to tell a similar story to Jablonski – that 'we are all one people'.[17] By analysing DNA from people from all corners of the world, Wells and his team discovered that all humans alive today are descended from a single man (Y-chromosomal Adam), who lived in Africa around 60,000 to 90,000 years ago, and from a single woman (mitochondrial Eve), who lived in Africa approximately 150,000 years ago.[18] (It's a quirk of our genetic evolution that our two most common recent ancestors did not have to live at the same time.)

Due to this common ancestry, the human genetic code, or genome, is 99.9 per cent identical, which suggests that the 0.1 per cent remainder that is responsible for our individual physical differences – skin colour, eye colour, hair colour and texture, etc. – has primarily been caused by environmental factors. Like Jablonski, Wells believes our early ancestors embarked on their first epic journey out of Africa in search of food, which led them to scatter gradually across the Earth. Wells explains that the physical appearance of these early travellers changed depending on which part of the world they migrated to. Those who ended up in Europe – in the northern hemisphere – received less sunlight, so their bodies did not need to produce as much melanin (a natural-forming skin pigment that protects from the sun's ultraviolet rays), and they developed lighter skin and straighter hair to match their new, colder conditions. The same is true for other communities around the world whose appearance adapted to match their new environment. And so our physical differences – once just mutations of survival – became embedded in our

DNA, to be passed down through the generations for millennia.

Wells's deep understanding of human DNA has also influenced his views on humanity and the false social construct of race. In an interview with the UK's *Independent* newspaper, he commented: 'It's worth getting the message out, that we are related to one another, that we are much more closely related genetically than people may suspect from glancing around and looking at these surface features that distinguish us . . . Race, in terms of deep-seated biological differences, doesn't exist scientifically'.[19]

Many of us have instinctively felt and argued for a long time that the concept of 'race' is a misleading human construct used to divide us, but it's reassuring to now have the science to back this up. If more of us understood the epic voyage that our early ancestors embarked upon, which led to the rich diversity we see around us today and paved the way for modern immigration, perhaps we wouldn't be so fixated on race. Indeed, we really are all one, and that oneness began in Africa.

The daily reality

Sadly, this understanding hasn't yet reached everyone. Even when young black men and women play by the 'rules' today, some find that many of the people they come across are still unable to see their academic and career achievements, but have less difficulty seeing their skin colour. Regardless of their personal journey, many young black people, mainly men, learn to take the stop-and-searches in their stride (after all, it's nothing new), as long as it results in their walking away – not something, as we've seen, that can be taken for granted. At work, he is frustrated with his lack of progress in relation to his contribution, although he is careful in office environments to mask his feelings for fear of being viewed as 'angry', 'threatening' or potentially violent. And she may have qualifications but is unable to get a foothold in the sector she has trained for, or has been given an opportunity and is expected to feel grateful while she remains at entry level and is surpassed by other colleagues, some of whom may be less qualified.

This is the reality for young black people, although it's fair to say that being prepared for the possibility of rejection on account of your colour from an early age does foster determination and can lead to success, as it forces one to develop astounding levels of resilience. Like diamonds, this pressurized environment can produce spectacular gems, such as Frederick Douglass, Rosa Parks, Martin Luther King, Muhammad Ali, Condoleezza Rice, Colin Powell, Michelle and Barack Obama, Kofi Annan, Oprah Winfrey, Sir David Adjaye, Toni Morrison, Ozwald Boateng OBE and many of the great men and women of colour who have helped shape our world for the better. However, it can also cause deep-rooted feelings of inferiority and inadequacy. The sense of never fully being accepted doesn't go away, especially as it is reinforced daily, which continuously erodes a sense of belonging and self-worth. For some black men in particular this can result in the rejection of education and the world of work, and lead to the pursuit of validation from a sub-culture where material possessions are valued above those things deemed further out of reach, such as employment and schooling. This route can indeed bring more immediate rewards than academia and employment, where rejection will already have been experienced, but it stands in the way of true social mobility.

Young males in poorer black communities can also fall prey to the trappings of a prescribed form of masculinity that thrives in these subcultures: one in which using violence to defend your reputation is seen as acceptable and sometimes necessary. Men in these environments – gangs, particularly – are often considered weak by their peers if they fail to defend their honour or respond to a slight, the consequences of which can be disastrous. Ironically, the ability to reason oneself out of conflict or to avoid it altogether would be applauded outside of the subculture but is often seen within the community as cowardice. And the rewards within the subculture – respect and attractiveness to women – are hard to refuse, especially if escaping the subculture is not seen as a possibility, which makes it pretty difficult to bring about a change in behaviour.

For many black men, this route leads to only one destination: in America especially there is a revolving door from the classroom to the prison cell. Mass incarceration has reached epic proportions, with one in three black men imprisoned at some point during their lives.[20] US prison populations would decline by 50 per cent if African Americans and Hispanics were incarcerated in the same proportion as white people.[21] This has big implications for their futures; the ramifications of a criminal record can be catastrophic for employment prospects and, once the step along the criminal-justice path has been taken, it's near impossible to turn back. Likewise, knife crime offences in 2019 rose to the highest level since 2011 in England and Wales, putting thousands of young black men on a pipeline to prison.[22]

When it comes to the American criminal-justice system, the odds are stacked against you if you are black. A 2016 report by The National Registry of Exonerations found that 47 per cent of all wrongful convictions involved black defendants. The figures for serious crimes such as murder show that black defendants account for 40 per cent of those convicted, but 50 per cent of those *wrongfully* convicted (in comparison to whites, who account for 36 per cent of those wrongfully convicted for murder). It's a similar picture with sexual assault: 59 per cent of all wrongful convictions were black defendants, compared with 34 per cent for white defendants.[23]

As well as falling victim to police brutality disproportionately, US blacks are also more likely to be victims of police misconduct, such as 'hiding evidence, tampering with witnesses or perjury'. This may also have contributed to the aforementioned racial disparity; the report concluded that black defendants accounted for 76 per cent of wrongful murder convictions in which police misconduct was involved, in comparison to 63 per cent of white exonerees.[24]

Ava DuVernay's powerful BAFTA-winning Netflix documentary *13th* chronicles how the abolition of slavery and the subsequent exploitation of the 13th Amendment, which deemed it unconstitutional to hold a person as a slave, has led to more black men being locked up now than there ever were during slavery. On the surface, the 13th Amendment seemed honourable and straightforward enough. But there was a loophole that excluded 'criminals', and so began the hyper-criminalization of the black male as a means of maintaining the free labour that had been so easily available during the years of slavery. It was not the first time the powers that be had found a loophole to assist their subjugation of black people. When the Constitution of the United States was drafted, the population of each state had to be calculated so that it could be given the appropriate number of representatives. But what about slaves? It was decided that only three in five slaves would count as people for the purposes of this process, in something that came to be known as the Three-Fifths Compromise. This gave the southern states

more seats in the House of Representatives, v.
turn allowed them to continue their industrialized en.
ment and helped to entrench a deep-down belief th.
black people are only three-fifths human.

This dehumanization continues today, and the loophole
created by the 13th Amendment has also morphed to fit
the times: from the Jim Crow laws of segregation to
mandatory sentencing and Nixon's 'war on drugs', from
Reagan's 'war on crime' to Clinton's Three-Strikes Law,
150 years of systematic discriminatory policy-making has
led us to the black-male-mass-incarceration epidemic in
the USA today.

American lawyer and founder of the Equal Justice
Initiative, Bryan Stevenson, has spent the best part of three
decades fighting to highlight the plight of those caught
in the crosshairs of the US criminal-justice system, and
he argues that the crux of the problem is how we treat
the marginalized and dispossessed:

*Proximity has taught me some basic and humbling truths,
including this vital lesson: each of us is more than the
worst thing we've ever done. My work with the poor and
the incarcerated has persuaded me that the opposite of
poverty is not wealth; the opposite of poverty is justice.
Finally, I've come to believe that the true measure of our
commitment to justice, the character of our society, our
commitment to the rule of law, fairness, and equality cannot
be measured by how we treat the rich, the powerful, the
privileged, and the respected among us. The true measure*

icter is how we treat the poor, the disfavoured,
, the incarcerated, and the condemned.[25]

so states that the criminal-justice system
irs those who are 'rich and guilty' over those
or and innocent' – after all, the poor can't
afford a good defence lawyer. It seems prison-for-profit
is a very lucrative business and is now a booming industry
– it pays to send people to prison. One of the final acts
of the Obama administration was to issue a memo to
bring an end to the Justice Department's reliance on
private prisons (which now account for approximately
18 per cent of US federal prisons – a figure that is steadily
increasing). The memo, issued by former Deputy Attorney
General Sally Yates, cited more 'safety and security incidents' in private prisons than public ones as the reason
for this change in policy. Unfortunately, a month after
Trump took the Oval Office in 2017 his Attorney General
at the time, Jeff Sessions, rescinded this and announced a
reinstatement of private prisons.

This, coupled with the fact that a whopping 90 to 95
per cent of prisoners accept a plea bargain and never go
to trial, has created a system where poor people of colour
are disproportionately incarcerated.[26] This is not only
ethically wrong but also, in the long term, economically
insane. To discard one-third of all black males when they
are in their prime and most able to contribute to society
is a cataclysmic dent in the moral, social and economic
fabric of America.

The double struggle

It is not just black men who find themselves disadvantaged because of prejudice. The fight for gender equality often crosses over into, and sometimes clashes with, the fight for racial equality, and black women are at the epicentre of these two struggles. They have to fight on two fronts: they must negotiate a society that discriminates against them because of their colour and sex, and also imposes upon them a standard of female beauty that is at the other end of the spectrum of what they represent. In a patriarchal society, women are judged primarily by their appearance before they even say or do anything. It is in this context that we find the labels of the 'strong black woman' who overcomes opposition and adversity, and the 'angry black woman' who is loud and unreasonable.

But before we resort to labels, we should examine the details of the black female experience more closely. Black women raised in the USA and UK will soon become aware that they were not meant to be the delicate damsel rescued by the hero. In fact, in order to be worthy of acceptance they need to become as close as they can manage to their white counterparts by suppressing the essence of their authenticity, i.e. their 'blackness'. Black females in corporate front-of-house roles are often told that their natural Afro hair or braided styles are unacceptable, and that chemical treatments or weaves and wigs that give the appearance of straighter hair are preferable. And even then, wigs and weaves can become a means of denigration, as black US congresswoman Maxine Waters found when political commentator Bill O'Reilly of Fox News claimed he 'couldn't hear what she was saying because of her James Brown wig'.

Waters responded defiantly as a 'strong black woman who cannot be intimidated or undermined'. She also made a rallying statement to *all* women: 'Don't allow these right-wing talking heads, these dishonourable people, to intimidate you or scare you. Be who you are. Do what you do. And let us get on with discussing the real issues of this country'.[27] The congresswoman's response resonated with many professional black women around the world, who tweeted stories of routine and systemic disrespect at work, ranging from having their authority undermined to being mocked over their appearance. The hashtag #blackwomenatwork trended on Twitter. These jibes may appear like harmless humour to some, but in actual fact they're an acute reminder of the real power relationship in the workplace in a society where black women have always been at the bottom of the hierarchy. As a black woman in the media, I have my own wounds and scars from some of the prejudice, rejection and subtle slights I have faced throughout my career. I learned very early on that the rules were not the same for me and that my point of difference, although an asset in most cases, was also sometimes a liability.

One incident that comes to mind was when I was around twenty-one. I had not long been at MTV, yet had one of the highest-rated shows on the network: *MTV*

Dancefloor Chart. I was succeeded by Russell Brand when I went to co-present *MTV Select* with British comedian Richard Blackwood. It was a great time in the channel's history – I was part of a wave of MTV VJs (video jockeys) that included Cat Deeley, Edith Bowman, Donna Air and Sara Cox. We were young, hip and the voice of Generation X. MTV had just newly rebranded in the UK and Ireland, and the network comms team embarked on an extensive marketing campaign to promote the faces of the channel. This involved a *SKY Magazine* cover titled 'MmmmTV . . . Delicious Reasons to Watch MTV'. The cover was a substantial beauty spread that included every female MTV presenter, except me – even though, at the time, my show was riding high in the ratings and I was a firm favourite with the viewers. My heart sank as I walked past news-stands and saw the cover glaring at me. I was happy for my colleagues but couldn't help crying at the fact that I'd been excluded.

What happened next completely raised my spirits, though. Because it was such a big cover story, the viewers of MTV started calling the network to ask if I had left the channel. The news soon spread that I hadn't left; I just hadn't been included in the shoot. It would later transpire that it wasn't *SKY Magazine* that had vetoed me – rather, it was the MTV PR team, who didn't think I was right for the feature so hadn't put my name forward. I am a glass-half-full type of person and always look for the silver lining where possible. This rejection, painful as it was, ended up working in my favour – more and more viewers kept calling the MTV switchboard to complain. As a result, the MTV press office devised a marketing campaign specifically for me, and I ended up shooting a piece for *SKY Magazine* with the legendary photographer David Bailey. As they say, when life gives you lemons – make lemonade!

However, incidents such as these would continue throughout my career. Many times I would agree to a cover shoot only to be bumped off at the last minute – something fuelled by the general unspoken belief in the industry that women of colour do not sell magazines, which, as demonstrated by Italian *Vogue*'s bestselling 'Black' issue, clearly isn't the case.

It's fair to say that women of colour have a double dose of discrimination: we are often ignored and excluded or, worse still, insulted in the media – and sometimes that insult is at the hands of our colleagues.

Such was the case for stalwart Labour MP Diane Abbott, following the Article 50 vote in 2017 that awarded Conservative Prime Minister Theresa May the authority to begin the process of leaving the European Union. The Brexit Minister David Davis allegedly attempted to hug Abbott for voting with the government, but apparently her response to his show of affection was a strong verbal rejection. Davis then proceeded to inform a 'friend' about this exchange via text, remarking that he would have to be blind to hug Diane Abbott. Fortunately, this 'friend' leaked Davis's text to the press. As hurtful as this was for Abbott, it was important that Davis's disgraceful disrespect was exposed for all to see. No doubt critics on the other side of this argument will claim that this was merely a joke, and that chastising David Davis is just another case of political correctness. Well, in this and many other cases, politics needs correcting, as too many women, especially those of us who are black, have been expected to tolerate 'jokes' that men would not want directed at their wives, daughters or sisters. This very public example of misogyny in the workplace helped shine a spotlight on the ways in which black women are stereotyped and denigrated on a daily basis.

This treatment can prompt a heightened sensitivity, especially when your experiences have taught you that this type of unfair abuse can come from anywhere at any time. With no expectation of being defended by wider society, many of us are left with no choice but to defend ourselves, sometimes robustly, hence the term 'angry black woman', which is propagated in the media and society generally. This can be the case even when we have broken barriers and succeeded against all odds, whether it is Michelle Obama being branded an 'ape',[28] or Venus Williams being called a 'gorilla',[29] or Viola Davis deemed 'less classically beautiful' by the *New York Times*.[30]

I once unwittingly found myself witness to a media firestorm around the issue of the so-called 'angry black woman'. As a regular presenter for Sky TV, I was asked by their PR team to moderate a panel for the premiere of the TV show *Guerrilla*, which was soon airing on Sky Atlantic. *Guerrilla* is a story about the British Black Power movement, and the panel included the Oscar-winning writer–producer John Ridley, actor–producer Idris Elba and other cast members who were taking questions from an invite-only audience. Members of the audience, including Dominique Hines from the *Express* newspaper, organizer Imani Robinson and activist Wail Qasim, questioned Ridley on why he had decided to cast an Indian woman (Freida Pinto) rather than a black woman as the female lead. His response was that historically Asian women had been prominent in the UK Black Power movement; this is true and was corroborated by audience member Neil Kenlock, the official photographer of the Black Panther group in Britain. Ridley then went on to explain that he had also been an activist in an interracial relationship, just like the show's lead character, and had also received prejudice from some in the African American community. The black women and men in the audience argued back and accused Ridley of 'black erasure', meaning he had chosen to disregard the contributions of black women in the movement.

Freida Pinto became visibly upset at the questioning of her casting, and the media story the following day was that aggressive Black Lives Matter activists had reduced her to tears.[31] Great for reinforcing the image of the angry black female, but not so great for addressing the pertinent issue of the representation of black women in the media. As a black woman, I understand that history and experience can make us focus our frustrations where it helps us least. I understand how it feels as a black woman to have your contributions overlooked in the media, in the professional world and in history in general – the visceral feeling of humiliation yet again as your role in a story is demoted or 'erased'. But challenging the creative licence of a writer to tell a story in the way they want to is the fight that reinforces the stereotype.

The wider argument is about the representation of Black Asian and Multi-Ethnic individuals in the creative industries, rather than in one piece of work. I would have liked to see that passion directed towards industry gatekeepers, and for them to have been challenged to open up more meaningful opportunities for diverse creatives. David Olusoga's 2020 McTaggart Lecture at The Edinburgh TV Festival did this brilliantly and powerfully by honestly calling out the systemic racism that has existed for far too long in the media industry:

I've been given amazing opportunities, but I've also been patronised and marginalised. I've been in high demand, but I've also been on the scrap heap. I've felt inspired, and convinced that our job – making TV and telling stories – is the best job in the world. But at other times I've been so crushed by my experiences, so isolated and disempowered by the culture that exists within our industry, that I have had to seek medical treatment for clinical depression. I've come close to leaving this industry on several occasions. And I know many black and brown people who have similar stories to tell.

…There are consequences of always being in a minority of one. Always being in a minority of one, fighting every fight alone, seeing what others don't see, all of this takes its toll. My own history of depression testifies to that.[32]

Olusoga went on to lament the lost generation of diverse creatives who have either left for America or given up on the industry altogether. I understand this frustration first-hand, as I too felt compelled to move to America to advance my career. In the end, though, I came back to Britain because it is my home and the country I love, and I wanted to be part of the solution in changing the creative industry for the better. Creating real change was also a key focus within Olusoga's address. In order to do this, we all need to be involved in making sure there is increased diversity in the rooms where projects are greenlit. This is something that I am committed to in my capacity as Global Director of Creative Diversity for the BBC.

Michelle Obama eloquently discussed the issue of being labelled as an angry black protestor with Oprah Winfrey in her final TV interview before leaving the White House. When she addressed how she dealt with being called an 'angry black woman' in her early days as First Lady, and how she rose above this to change the hearts and minds of America and show the world who she really was, she told Oprah, 'I don't hold on to the bad stuff. As black women, there's so much that comes at us all the time, every day, in subtle ways that could tear your soul apart if you let it. My mother taught me: you better keep it moving. You have to brush it off'.[33]

She is completely right that one has to adopt an extra layer of resilience in order to deal with this kind of discrimination. The one benefit of not receiving adequate or equal validation from the outside world is that it means you go inside yourself to draw upon your own self-esteem, and, in the end, that is the only thing you can truly rely on anyway. This applies to *all* women. When we learn to feel good about ourselves in spite of what the outside world might say, eventually that level of authentic confidence, whatever your gender or skin colour, is undeniable and the outside world finally follows suit. It's infectious – we all know it when we see it and can't help but want to be around it. In the end, self-love and self-acceptance trump sexism and racism.

Yes, we can!

Clearly, these stories are not the experience of every black man or woman. The majority will play by rules that are stacked against them and will seek inclusion, complete their education and make sacrifices by going the extra mile, conforming to a mainstream culture, and focusing on presenting an acceptable and 'unthreatening' outward appearance, harbouring dreams that this will help people to concentrate on the content of their character as opposed to their colour.

Having lived in America for eight years, I consider it my second home – and a paradox. In one country, we see dreams and aspirations realized that would be impossible anywhere else. But we also see that the fear and division from the 'original sin' of slavery remains.

For me, the election of the first African American president was a watershed in American and global history, akin to the election of Nelson Mandela. I count myself privileged to have played a small civic part in the Obama election campaign, canvassing on the eve of the election in Virginia – a deep red Republican state that had not been blue since Lyndon B. Johnson's victory in 1964. And even though LBJ won the state back then, many white residents in Virginia were against his landmark civil-rights legislation and had wanted to keep segregation after that point. Virginia would never again be a true-blue state. Or so it seemed.

I had flown out to Virginia with my friends, Labour party strategists Baroness Margaret McDonagh and Anji Hunter. At campaign headquarters, I was struck by an elderly white gentleman whose face was badly bruised. Feeling concerned, I walked over to check if he was OK and asked how he had injured himself. With a voice full of emotion, this southern gentleman revealed to me that he was in his nineties and owned a farm that had been in his family for generations. He had fallen over a few days before and had hurt his face on a rake. But, against doctor's orders, he was determined to come and support the Obama campaign efforts.

He explained to me how, as a young man, he had been an ardent segregationist and saw his backing of Obama's election as a route to some sort of redemption. He never thought he would live to see an African American president but felt he needed to actively support Obama in order to right some of the wrongdoings of his past. After speaking to this gentleman, I felt something momentous was about to happen. That evening, Margaret and I attended the final Obama rally in Virginia. It was a cool, crisp night, and the atmosphere was electric as we all sensed history was about to be made.

The then Senator Obama had just lost his grandmother, who had died that day in Hawaii, so he was flown in by helicopter to the rally. There wasn't a dry eye in the house as he paid homage to his grandmother, Toot, and the vital role she had played in helping to shape him as a man. He went on to explain the origins of his campaign slogan, 'Fired Up, Ready to Go', which we all were as we left this poignantly magical evening.

The next day, Margaret, Anji and I watched the election results at the home of legendary Democratic pollster and close Clinton confidant Stan Greenberg. His DC townhouse was heaving with guests, many of whom were close allies of the Clintons.

Everyone was jubilant as the results started coming in and it began to look like victory was on the horizon. Once Ohio was called, we knew it was game over. Everyone began cheering – then, we all sat in silence as we watched the footage of the victorious Obamas and Bidens take the stage in Grant Park Chicago, with Oprah and Jesse Jackson shedding tears of joy in the crowd.

As Anji, Margaret and I left Stan Greenberg's house, we were met with cheering and dancing in the streets of Washington. Cars were beeping their horns, Obama 2008 signs were everywhere and a joyful crowd was roaring 'Yes We Can'. The atmosphere was like the home-coming of a winning Superbowl team multiplied tenfold. America was proud of itself because, in that moment, it had decided to look beyond its complex issues with race and chosen 'change' and 'hope' over the status quo. In doing so, they had done something that, in all likelihood, no other Western country would have been capable of at the time. This is the dream personified by the Obama presidency, which was both an inspiration and a post-racial challenge to young black people everywhere. If Obama can do it, why can't you? When the system is inherently stacked against you, this is easier said than done.

In the UK, this certainly seems to be the case. A study conducted as part of a BBC documentary hosted by British actor David Harewood examined the probability of the UK ever having a black prime minister. Using empirical evidence to project how likely it would be for male children from different backgrounds to make it to the nation's highest electoral office, the findings were shocking, to say the least. Statistically, a black child born in the UK has a 1 in 17 million chance of becoming prime minister, while a white child has a 1 in 1.4 million chance, and a white child with a private education and a degree from Oxford University has a 1 in 200,000 chance.[34] What this effectively means is that we are severely restricting the talent pool for political leadership, and rebirthing the same ideas and thought patterns again and again.

This presents numerous issues, perhaps the most concerning being that by completely excluding 'other' talent pools from the decision-making process, the changes that many of us seek become even more unlikely. With few exceptions, it seems that whichever side of the political aisle they sit on, most of the leaders available to us have all trodden the same path and share a similar world-view. It seems pretty clear that in order for there to be sustainable change, the people leading us need to change, too. But in order for this to happen, education and employment opportunities for young black people need to be put in place – in contrast to what, currently, is often endemic poverty and lack of opportunity.

Because in reality, regardless of the data suggesting that the odds are heavily stacked against a black person becoming president or prime minister, the truth is that most don't want to anyway. The dreams and aspirations of black people are no different to the dreams and aspirations of anyone else – the difference is that many will have a shortage of realistic role models in the media or within their own families, people who have been supported by the education system, and have been able to work hard, attain the right training or qualifications, prove the right to 'belong' and be rewarded accordingly. For the ambitious, hard-working black person, this unlevel playing field can be extremely demoralizing. A black person ends up asking: am I the problem? Is it my colour, or am I simply not good enough? Am I one of those people with a chip on my shoulder, imagining prejudice?

Nina Jablonski believes that a new form of education and honest dialogue is needed to turn back this tide of hundreds of years of misunderstanding and mistrust, and I wholeheartedly agree. She argues that endemic racism is holding back not just black people, but the whole of society:

Erroneous and deep-seated notions about race persist because we are scared to discuss misconceptions about colour and race in our classrooms and boardrooms. Paranoia about race born of political correctness has led to the perpetuation of misconceptions about colour and race, the cloaking of discriminatory behaviour and language, and the persistence of racism. Racism is probably humanity's single biggest impediment to human achievement.[35]

The transatlantic slave trade is now a thing of the past and, thankfully, society has moved on in the last century. We now have antidiscrimination policies and legislation in place, and yet clearly these are not doing enough, as the repercussions of our unexamined past are still being felt to this day. The stats prove that a young black person still rarely sees him- or herself reflected in any positions of seniority. A black parent can only hope that things will be better for their child – a tangible hope, as things are certainly better than they were for his or her parents. But hope may not be enough. Jablonski is not alone in demanding real, substantial change. 'Race at the Top', a comprehensive study by Race for Opportunity on BAME representation in leadership in UK business, concluded that there had been virtually no ethnicity change in top management positions in British business in the five years between 2007 and 2012.[36] In a letter to the British government, Sandra Kerr – the CEO of Race for Opportunity – urged them to deal with this problem as a matter of urgency before it was too late:

By 2051, one in five people in the UK will be from an ethnic minority background, representing a scale of consumer spending and political voting power that business and government alike cannot afford to ignore. The gap must not be allowed to widen further, but without action little will change. I am calling on government for a review to amplify understanding around the barriers BAME employees face in reaching management positions, and for two simple words – 'and race' – to be added to the UK Corporate Governance Code. We urgently need this to happen if we are to ensure that we don't pass the point of no return.[37]

If governments heed such stark warnings, if we can undo the centuries of false racial programming and teach our children the scientific truth of our common ancestry and foster a wealth of role models for young black people at home and in the media, then maybe, just maybe, the achievements of someone like Barack Obama can become the standard, rather than the exception to the rule.

The rise of extremism and white supremacy

In the last few years, there has been an alarming rise in far-right extremism and white-supremacist groups. Who could forget the horror of 16 June 2016, when the MP Jo Cox was murdered by far-right-extremist Thomas Mair, shouting 'Britain first'? Before his wife was murdered, Brendan Cox had actually been studying this frightening trend. Speaking a year after Jo's passing at the 2017

Amnesty International General Meeting, he warned of the grave challenge facing us and issued a clarion call to all those who believe in a fair and inclusive society:

We are facing a new threat today – one that we still haven't fully appreciated. We have got into the absurd position of celebrating fascists coming second in national elections, rather than first, as if that is a great outcome.

I'm not suggesting that we become defeatist, but unless we are clear about the size and scale of the challenge, we will be defeated by it . . .

The threat of rising far-right extremism is real and it isn't going to go away quickly. But with resolution, a concerted attempt to reach out, and a focus on building closer communities, we can and we will defeat it.[38]

These so-called 'populist' leaders have manipulated and exploited the genuine concerns of people who are witnessing their traditional way of life evaporating in front of their eyes, and who haven't been given the right tools to adapt to this change. Fuelled by a 'cause conspiracy' ignited by the dangerous rhetoric of a new breed of charismatic social-media-savvy demagogues, there has been an exponential increase in far-right membership and incidents. In the UK alone, the 'suspected far-right extremists flagged to the government's key anti-terror programme recently soared by 30 per cent over twelve months'.[39]

Having a cause to get behind is one of the most powerful of all callings, especially for men who are often lacking in words and therefore prefer action. 'Other' young men who are excluded due to race, class or religion are all the more vulnerable to radicalization and the rhetoric of causes, which will supposedly give their lives greater significance while at the same time putting them in jeopardy.

America is facing its own issues with a rise in white-supremacy movements. Having experienced first-hand the uplifting feeling of unity in Virginia during Obama's 2008 election, watching the clashes between the far-right extremists and antiracism protesters in Charlottesville on the news in 2017 filled me with dread; it felt like America had gone back in time, to racial tensions and the strife of the Sixties. We had reverted to arguing over whether to celebrate Confederate generals who fought to keep slavery. We were, once again, seeing the KKK marching with lit torches – only this time the marchers were brazen enough to do so without hoods.

President Trump took forty-eight hours to condemn the violence of the white-supremacist protesters in Charlottesville and the senseless murder of thirty-two-year-old Heather Hayer, an antiracism protester, at the hands of James Alex Fields Jr, a far-right extremist and domestic terrorist.[40] This dangerous, overt racism must be challenged. Realistic solutions that allow everyone to thrive in the modern world are needed, rather than a return to an older, more racist and less progressive America. The country has come too far to turn back now.

If the rise of extremism and white supremacy are the products of disaffection among white people in lower socioeconomic groups, it is also important to consider how that same resentment manifests in more affluent white males. As the march towards inclusion progresses, in some more middle-class circles there is an undercurrent of resentment brewing. I co-host *The Pledge*, a weekly debate show, for Sky News in the UK. The format of the show requires each panel member to select a pressing topic to bring to *The Pledge* table for discussion. For International Men's Day in 2018, my fellow panellist, author and journalist Rachel Johnson (sister of the British Prime Minister Boris Johnson), chose a racial and gender discrimination case with a difference.

In May 2018, Jo Wallace, the newly appointed Creative Director of ad agency J. Walter Thompson, took to the stage alongside her colleague Lucas Peon, Executive Creative Director, at a Creative Equals diversity summit in London. She proudly announced to the excited audience that she was a 'gay woman' who planned to 'obliterate' JWT's repu-tation as a 'Knightsbridge boys' club'. Some considered Wallace's remarks a real breakthrough and an apt response to the recent revelations that JWT had the worst gender pay gap in advertising, a difference of 44.7 per cent in favour of men. These startling statistics were described by Peon as 'really, really horrible'. 'In the World Cup of sucking at pay-gap numbers, we made the final', he said.

It seemed the two colleagues were in sync on the issue. In fact, the whole agency was, having previously released a statement vowing to radically address the overall lack of diversity within the company, as well as the disparity in pay between its male and female employees. However, not everyone was on side. Wallace's comments in particular hit a raw nerve with a small group of white male executives who expressed their concerns to the human-resources department, questioning what the implications of her words meant for them and their careers. According to reports, days later these white men were sacked.

News of their dismissal spread like wildfire, sparking a polarized response both internally and within the ad industry at large. Advertising veteran and equality campaigner Cindy Gallop came to Wallace's defence and condemned the men: 'It's the perfect example of, as the saying goes, "When you are used to privilege, equality feels like oppression."' However, former JWT insiders warned that the company risked 'swapping one form of racism for another' in the rush to address long-standing diversity problems: 'If someone had stood up on the stage and said it's our ambition to purge JWT of young black lesbians, we'd be on the front page of the papers, and rightly so'.

The company would indeed end up on the front pages when the dismissed men sought legal representation to investigate the viability of an unfair dismissal case on the basis of race and gender discrimination. Their lawyer Adrian Scotland, managing partner at Judge Sykes Frixou, declined to talk about the specifics for legal reasons but predicted that discrimination cases brought by straight white men would become increasingly common as companies increase diversity and close their gender pay gaps:

> *I cannot discuss the specifics of the reported dispute at JWT. Speaking generally . . . over the past twelve months or so a new phenomenon has emerged. Ordinary people from a wide variety of employment are coming to me for advice, as they are feeling targeted simply because they are white, heterosexual and male. This is happening across multiple sectors, including financial services, advertising, higher education and the public sector. It is resulting in a growing distrust of the diversity industry. The idea that a white straight man in this country could be a victim in any way is almost seen as reprehensible.*

Rachel Johnson argued that this case was symbolic of a wider issue relating to resentment brewing among some straight white men and that the inclusion movement needed to craft a narrative that achieved the very thing it purports to promote: inclusion. This also means 'including' straight white men, otherwise this unchecked resentment could impede the change and progress we all need. I agreed with her 100 per cent and fully supported her in the debate. As Adrian Scotland told *The Pledge*: 'The fundamental purpose of equality initiatives should be to increase tolerance and improve unity across our diverse society. It is sadly ironic that these progressive initiatives appear to be being implemented in such a regressive fashion. I fear it will result in a backlash'.

I think Adrian Scotland makes a very valid point. We cannot replace one form of discrimination for another, no matter how well intentioned. What we must instead do is adopt a fresh approach that includes everyone, even those who up until now have benefitted disproportionately. If we continue with the scarcity mindset that has governed society for so long, then invariably the response will be one of fear. The dog-eat-dog approach, where my win means your loss, will do nothing but divide us further. However, if we instead choose to think differently and opt for a more abundant outlook, working together to build something that is greater than the sum of its parts, then the result could be growth and collective success like none we have never seen.

Now is the time for white people in the twenty-first century who want to be a part of the solution, who feel compelled to undo some of the injustices of the past by helping to shape the type of society that nurtures the talents of all its citizens, to stand up and step up. This requires two questions to be answered: how? And, more importantly: why? When the odds are stacked in your favour, it's hard to comprehend what life is like for those whom the odds are stacked against; when a system is built to facilitate your advancement, it's hard to imagine what it feels like for those the system was designed to fail. It might be hard to imagine, but it is not impossible and it's vital if we are to create the type of society that is free from division and civil unrest, the type of society that allows all of its citizens to fulfil their potential.

A FAIRER FUTURE –
THE ACTIONS

History is not the past. History is the present. We carry our history with us.

James Baldwin

Action One

Achieve awareness

According to racism scholar and author Ibram X. Kendi there can be no gray area when it comes to racism, one is either racist (even if inadvertently so) or actively anti-racist. There is no such thing as a 'non-racist.' Therefore, in order to overcome the consequences of the historical pursuit of power by those who have shared your white identity, you first need to understand and accept the reality of the impact this legacy has had on 'others' who do not share all of your elevated characteristics. This means achieving awareness of the contextual journey of individuals who have not been operating on a level playing field. This knowledge will provide you with a balanced perspective and a deeper appreciation of the building blocks of inequality. Understanding the very foundations of discrimination will in turn help you to select the appropriate tools to dismantle the pillars of injustice.

The best way to start is by getting a first-hand account of the challenges 'others' face, and by becoming a committed listener and a passionate observer of the unequal reality faced by people of colour in our society. However, watching and listening is not enough – actions do indeed speak louder than words, so it is also important to become a motivated advocate and ally of black people. This is easier said than done, of course, especially when you are not personally affected by racism. The way forward here is to accept that there are alternative realities and experiences to your own, in which talent, potential and opportunity are denied, suppressed or even excluded.

I would highly recommend watching on YouTube a riveting dialogue between leading thought-agitators Cornel West and Chris Hedges. Hedges really explains the limitations of privilege:

Privilege blinds you. Those of us who come out of privilege, if we're going to be intellectually and finally morally effective and honest, it's about ripping away the blinders of privilege.

Even so:

> As hard as you try, when you come out of a position of
> privilege as an American, as a Caucasian, as a male, that
> blindness is never, ever going to go away. So you have to
> struggle as much as you can, but then you have to honour
> the fact that there are things because of where you come
> from that you will never be able see. Therefore, you have
> to listen closely to the voices around you.[41]

To genuinely achieve this, you also need to challenge
your own view of reality, and even your ingrained and
unexamined feelings of superiority. One of the best ways
to do this is to scrutinize objective data. For instance, at
work look at who applies and who gets accepted/hired.
Examine employee exits and who makes it to positions
of seniority. What does your company's progression pipeline look like? If you notice a discrepancy among those
lacking elevated characteristics, then give that reality the
chance of being a hypothesis and investigate it further.
You can do this through mentoring an individual of a
different identity or by joining or supporting a network
or charity that specializes in addressing inequality based
on identity.

In the modern era, as established hierarchies have begun
to be challenged, ideas of straight white male supremacy
have in particular become divisive. This does not mean
there is no place for straight white men, or for white
people more generally, to participate in the change our

society needs to see, but they must first understand the origins of their flawed assumptions, the ones that have created the systemic inequality and barriers to inclusion that we see all around us. To gain this understanding, white people must be willing to adopt the attributes needed to be agents of change; for example, relinquishing the need to automatically go on the defensive when the issue of racism is raised. Instead, be open to listening to where your blind spots might be. Going on the attack immediately shuts down the kinds of conversations that can create breakthroughs.

I accept, however, that the case for change has not yet been fully accepted, and we are not all on the same page. Some of us feel left behind or not fully convinced of the direction we are moving in. Some may even wonder what a challenge to systemic racism and the creation of a more inclusive society means for their own interests – will there be some kind of retrospective payback, whereby white people are held accountable or victimized for past wrong-doings and the development of a system that they had no part in creating? That is not my intention. We must move away from guilt and blame, as they only lead to fear and not the action that we need to see.

Once you have informed yourself and understand how the system works, and how deeply entrenched it is – through education, advertising, the media – you will realize that undoing these limiting beliefs is no small feat, but it is vital if we are to build a better future. The truth is, this unfair system is preventing us as a whole from being as productive and successful as we can be, and it therefore needs to be amended for all of our sakes – this is the whole point of addressing our diversity and inclusion challenges.

I recognize and accept there are multiple struggles in incorporating the necessary changes, but we must try, and this requires the full cooperation of as many white people as possible. Without that involvement, progress will be impeded or, worse, attacked again and again.

Understandably, if you are white, straight and male and in a position of leadership, your lived experience and perception of the world is going to be different from mine. I'm sure you appreciate there is a degree of inequality in the world, but by and large you may be of the opinion that if a person works hard enough, then eventually their talents will win through. There are of course some non-whites, women and LGBTQ+ individuals in leadership positions to demonstrate this, but sadly they are the exception rather than the rule.

And it will not become the rule unless we all actively work to subvert the patterns and systems that are in place to ensure that if you aren't a white person – and most often a straight male as well – to reach senior leadership positions you need to be exceptional. By exceptional I don't mean that the person has a remarkable set of skills or attributes that sets them apart. I mean that they have been subject to a set of circumstances so different from the norm that it has set them apart from peers who share their identity. Barack Obama is a perfect example of this, a man classified by many as black (albeit with a white mother) who lived such a unique set of circumstances that they gave him a skillset and experiences that set him on a course to the presidency of the United States of America. We can no longer afford to rely on exceptional circumstances and leave examples like this to chance – rather, they must become the norm. We need all of us, but especially straight white men, to actively create the conditions that allows us to rectify a system that more or less guarantees the usual people succeed and the usual people fail. In order to do this, we must dedicate time and step out of our own realities as often as possible to see how the system works for or against 'others'.

One good way to do this is to read history written from a different perspective to the Western mainstream. I recommend books by David Olusoga, Robin Walker and Cheikh Anta Diop. (And see the end of the book for more suggestions of reading material that will expand your knowledge and understanding of the issues surrounding race.) The objective is to accept the extent to which the system and our own assumptions work to deliver the same results we have always had in terms of who is included and who isn't. Achieving awareness will go a long way to helping you comprehend how and why inequality exists, and enable you to become better placed to support interventions that subvert these patterns.

Action Two

Make a small step with a big footprint

Once we accept the power and privilege that accompanies white identity, and arm ourselves with knowledge about race inequality, the next step is to look at how this awareness can be used positively. At its most basic level, the involvement of white people in any push for inclusion helps to mainstream the matter, instead of it being considered a fringe interest for individuals of a particular identity. At the same time, small actions can make a big difference. Sometimes it can even be as simple as opening your front door. Take as an example the inspirational case of Reggie Nelson and Quintin Price.

In 2014, Reggie Nelson, a seventeen-year-old black man brought up on a council estate in Canning Town in east London, was at a loss as to what he wanted to do with his life. His father, an alcoholic, had recently died, and although Reggie had hoped to pursue a career in football, he decided that he needed something more reliable. But where to start? With no sense of how to access the support and information he would need to guide him, he took the unorthodox step of Googling 'richest area in London' and travelling on the tube to Kensington, where he proceeded to knock on doors and deliver a polite speech asking for advice.[42] He wanted to know what the inhabitants of some of London's wealthiest homes had done to get where they had. The response was, to say the least, mixed. Most people said they couldn't help, others offered generic words of encouragement and some slammed their doors in his face.

After persevering for a few hours, he got a lucky break. He rang the buzzer of the home of Quintin and Elizabeth Price, and found a couple who were really willing to listen to him. Quintin was at that time Head of Alpha Strategies at BlackRock, the world's largest investment company, and he returned from parking his car to find Elizabeth talking to Reggie after she had invited him in. Quintin explained what he did for a living and offered to help.

It would have been easy for the Prices to forget all about this encounter and continue as if it had never happened, but Quintin was true to his word and arranged for Reggie to attend a training day for undergraduates at BlackRock's headquarters in London in the spring. Reggie was then invited back for a week-long work-experience programme in the summer, after which Quintin spoke to him and his mum and encouraged Reggie to attend university, as well as offering his continued mentorship. Six years later and Reggie is now a Fiduciary Management Analyst at Legal & General Investment Management (LGIM). He is also Group Chair of the Association of Chartered Certified Accountants Emerging Talent Advisory Group and Founder of K3D, a social-mobility enterprise.

All Reggie needed was some direction and support to fulfil his amazing potential. The simple act of the Prices opening their door to him was enough for him to go on and do the hard work himself, and that small act of kindness and open-mindedness has created a ripple effect of inclusion, with Reggie now mentoring BAME candidates himself. This is something I've seen in my family with my own Reggie. After my auntie came to the UK from Ghana, she was befriended by an older white working-class couple from east London in a climate where there was potential for fear and hostility on both sides. In this instance, though, love and openness prevailed, and my cousin Reg – born into a culture different to his mother's – gained surrogate grandparents who cherished him and even helped to bridge the gap between him and my auntie. They provided the patience and time that a struggling single mother in a foreign land couldn't; the mother and her child provided a childless couple with the unconditional love and respect that was due to them in their twilight years. Reg came to understand both his African heritage and English culture, celebrating the best of both and understanding their challenges, too. As an adult, he has gone on to dedicate his working life to helping others in need, always going that extra mile. This couple's small act of inclusion thereby had a huge impact, with Reg passing on the spirit of openness that they helped foster in him.

But what about all of the others who do not have surrogate grandparents, or the courage to knock on strangers' doors? As Reggie Nelson says:

> There are so many talented individuals out there, who will never be able to have a fair crack at changing the trajectory of their life, simply because of a lack of opportunity. If we want to make society fairer and level the playing field, then we need to be ready to cast the net further and give these talented people a shot. When I give a talk at corporate institutions, I regularly hear 'we need more Reggies', and although this is humbling to hear, the truth is there are tons of people like me out there. It's just that they do not have the visibility to the opportunities and a lack of social capital. I had to literally knock on doors in order to obtain this visibility.[43]

And this is the point: we are missing out on a wealth of talent if we expect people like Reggie to knock on doors in order to have a chance at fulfilling their potential. It is now time for people in positions of privilege to not just be open to meeting and understanding the experiences of people from outside their privileged group but also to seek out Reggies and offer them the support and opportunities they need to make their valuable contributions to society. If we do this, we will all be better off.

This is something that Quintin recognizes from his own experience. He says:

When Reggie knocked on our door, Elizabeth and I both had experience of mentorship, and recognized the power of education in transforming people's lives. However, in my case, this was mainly within the context of my professional life, and the people I was mentoring already had their foot in the door. Reggie opened my eyes to the fact that there are countless other people out there who have the potential to succeed if they are presented with the right opportunities and advice. I am currently investigating a way to scale up in a systemized way the mentorship that I was able to offer Reggie so that we can reach many more kids who, like him, want the chance to achieve their ambitions. And in this way, I feel Reggie did more to change my life than I did his. He helped me to widen my perspective, and I am therefore very thankful that he came into my life.

This is the power of mentorship: it is a two-way street, with both parties benefiting from the exchange – a virtuous circle is created, demonstrating that inclusivity is win-win. And if everybody wins, the world can't help but be a better place.

Action Three

Build sustainable inclusivity

In order to build a sustainable future, the people who currently control the levers of wealth will need to make investment decisions with what I call 'share' values and impact at their heart, not just financial return. This can only be achieved with investment in social enterprises and initiatives that create sustainability by providing opportunities for marginalized groups to survive and thrive.

The recent charitable work of Melinda Gates is a great example of an ally using her wealth in a more inclusive way. Working in partnership with her husband Bill, their malaria charities have saved countless lives. And Pivotal Ventures, her venture-capital fund, specifically supports entrepreneurs from diverse identity groups, creating opportunity for individuals to achieve incredible things and potentially become wealth generators themselves. We must invest in the human value of sharing in this way, so that distributing wealth with a view towards a more sustainable balance across people of all identities becomes commonplace. This will lead to greater innovation and less poverty-fuelled conflict, reducing resentment and fear between the haves and have-nots.

Individuals can also play their part in creating this kind of sustainable inclusivity. In the weeks following the murder of George Floyd, many companies were quick to communicate messages of support for the Black Lives Matter cause, often via social media. In some cases, it seemed as though peer pressure to be seen to be doing the right thing, rather than a genuine engagement with the issues, was the true motivation behind these claims of solidarity. It is very easy to draft a corporate message of support; it is much harder to actually make a difference. Good intentions need to be backed up by action. If we as consumers choose to patronize businesses and companies that walk the walk, rather than just talking the talk, we can influence and force real change. How we consume can have a real impact.

One such company that has supported the Black Lives Matter movement since before the 2020 protests is Nike. In 2016, the successful American football player Colin Kaepernick, a quarterback for the San Francisco 49ers, decided to remain seated during the singing of the national anthem before a pre-season game. Afterwards, he said:

I am not going to stand up to show pride in a flag for a country that oppresses black people and people of colour. To me, this is bigger than football and it would be selfish on my part to look the other way. There are bodies in the street and people getting paid leave and getting away with murder.[44]

He went a step further before the start of the next game, and every other game that season, when he went down on one knee during the anthem, giving birth to the symbol of peaceful protest now known as 'taking a knee'. His actions, however, proved to be deeply contentious among certain sections of US society, and since being released by the 49ers after the 2016 season, he has been unable to find another team, leading to accusations that he has been blackballed from the NFL because of his political activism.[45] Even President Trump inevitably weighed in, condemning Kaepernick's actions and calling for him and other players who staged silent protests during the national anthem to be fired.[46]

Then, in 2018, Nike released a new advertising campaign with Kaepernick at its centre. Against a black-and-white close-up of his face were the words: 'Believe in something. Even if it means sacrificing everything'. The decision to support Kaepernick in such a high-profile way ultimately paid off, with an estimated $6 billion dollars added to the company's share price following the release of the ad, but it also had a positive social impact by amplifying his message around the world.[47] And it was not without its risks as a business strategy, as demonstrated by the videos on social media of people burning Nike goods.

While Nike, like any global company, has areas in which it can make further progress – for example, by making its products more environmentally sustainable, and by ensuring its workforce in developing countries are always paid a fair wage and provided with safe working conditions – they do take diversity and inclusion seriously. Census data shows that as of 2019 60.1 per cent of the US population identifies as white, with 39.9 per cent coming from underrepresented groups (URG).[48] This compares with 56.3 per cent of all Nike employees being made up of people from URGs, 24.6 per cent of Directors (up from 22.9 per cent in 2017) and 21.2 per cent of Vice Presidents (up from 15.6 per cent in 2017). There is obviously room for improvement in these figures, but Nike are committed to increasing representation further, particularly at the highest levels of the company: 'Our efforts to increase representation currently focus on the Vice President (VP) level, because representation at this level provides a foundation for us to grow representation at all levels'. And they also have a good track record on the important question of pay equity: for every $1 earned by white employees in the USA, people from URGs also earned $1.[49]

The BBC is another organization that is putting its money where its mouth is. In my role as Director of Creative Diversity, I was involved in securing a commitment by the BBC in June 2020 to invest £100 million of its existing commissioning budget over three years towards diverse and inclusive content, supported by a new mandatory 20 per cent diverse talent-target in all new network commissions from April 2021.[50] It is vitally important that the diversity in society is reflected in the content produced by a public-service broadcaster such as the BBC, and we as individuals can support this commitment to meaningful action by choosing to watch the BBC's programming, just as we can support a company such as Nike with our spending power. Through the choices we make as consumers, we can ensure it is the companies and organizations that implement positive change that are the ones who thrive, while those who pay lip-service to equality and social justice eventually fall by the wayside.

Action Four

Do the white/right thing

Standing up to injustice — whether in your workplace, community or even sometimes family — is not always easy, especially if you are part of the group that has created the conditions for that injustice to exist in the first place. However, if you want to be a modern ally and put your weight behind dismantling systemic racism, it is sometimes necessary to risk going against the prevailing view.

The Black Lives Matter protests in 2020 saw an unprecedented number of white people join in, both in the USA and around the world. Jesse Washington, a senior writer for *The Undefeated,* wrote:

Protests in hundreds of cities, in every state, have had large and sometimes majority-white crowds. White women made themselves human shields to protect black protesters. White superstar athletes, such as NFL quarterbacks Tom Brady and Joe Burrow, signed petitions and tweeted support. Utah's Republican Senator Mitt Romney joined *the cause. Apple committed $100 million to a racial justice fund; the NFL increased its commitment to $250 million. Museums and corporations supported the protests. Spontaneous reparations flowed. More than ever before in the movement that began with [Trayvon] Martin's killing in 2012, white people are chanting, posting, even screaming:* Black Lives Matter.[51]

It is difficult to pinpoint why this was the case. Perhaps it was down to the brutal and unambiguous nature of watching the eight-minutes-and-forty-six-second video of George Floyd's killing, making it impossible to ignore that racism is a systemic problem. The lockdown to combat the COVID-19 pandemic might also have contributed, with people around the world having stepped outside of their normal routines, allowing them to focus their attention on the atrocity in a way that would perhaps not have been possible when distracted by their daily lives and the fast-moving twenty-four-hour news cycle. Whatever the case, white people were very much involved in a way they hadn't been before. It was vital, however, that this wasn't a fleeting or performative participation. White people cannot take a stand only when it is fashionable to do so. Instead, a long-lasting, strategic involvement in the movement for change is required.

Consider what kind of person you want to be and what you want your legacy to be. If you want to be on the right side of history on this subject, it is vital that you engage in the process of challenging your white privilege in a sustained and meaningful way. Be mindful of your actions, and dare to be different, standing up for what is right, even when it is difficult to do so.

This was the philosophy of President Lyndon B. Johnson when he signed into US law the Civil Rights Act of 1964. Johnson understood how divisive inequality could be: 'If you can convince the lowest white man he's better than the best colored man, he won't notice you're picking his pocket. Hell, give him somebody to look down on, and he'll empty his pockets for you'.[52] He also knew that this historical legislative win would also mean a monumental loss for his Democratic Party. As white Southerners deserted the party in droves, Johnson remarked 'we have lost the South for a generation'. He was right: the Democrats did lose the South for generations. However, in the long term, this just Act included millions of African Americans in the democratic process and helped to redeem the moral standing of America in the eyes of the world. And Johnson was rewarded for doing the right thing, securing one of the biggest landslides in American history when he won the 1964 presidential election, even without the support of the Southern states.

In the UK, an event of similar magnitude occurred in 1999 when Sir William Macpherson published his report following the Stephen Lawrence Inquiry. Lawrence, a black teenager from south-east London, had been brutally murdered in 1993 in a racially motivated attack while waiting for a bus. The public inquiry was set up after accusations of mishandling of the initial investigation by the Metropolitan Police Service and the Crown Prosecution Service, which had seen five suspects being arrested but not charged. Macpherson concluded that the Met was 'institutionally racist' in a landmark moment for the criminal-justice system in the UK.[53] This admission by an establishment insider that systemic racism existed in the British police force was exactly the sort of honest and courageous act that is required for change to be possible. Regardless of the repercussions, you must be brave and call out racism whenever you see it, whether that be at the heart of British institutions such as the Met, or in your workplaces or everyday lives.

One way you can do this is by looking at your company's top leaders; this will tell you what it institutionally believes. If there is a lack of diversity, form a group of allies and raise this with the CEO, making it your mission to create change from within. An example of this within my own industry is the Black, Asian and Minority Ethnic TV Task Force, which was set up in the wake of George Floyd's killing to raise concerns about the way BAME people are treated in television, as well as to highlight the lack of representation, both on screen and behind the camera. Addressed to culture secretary Oliver Dowden, Ofcom, Pact, BBC, ITV, Channel 4, Channel 5, STV, Sky, UKTV, Netflix, Amazon and YouTube, and signed by more than 5,000 people, their open letter was a way of taking action in a visible way, even though the signatories might be at risk of being blacklisted or excluded.[54] If people of privilege can add their support to initiatives such as this one, even if it is uncomfortable for them to do so, the message will be amplified and change will become inevitable.

Action Five

Educate yourself about the past

As the 2020 BLM protests escalated around the world, statues of racist figures from the past quickly became a focus of attention. In the UK, the debate around statues and who we as a society choose to memorialize was brought into the foreground after the toppling of the statue in Bristol of slave trader Edward Colston. Similarly, following years of debate and controversy about the removal of statues to Confederate generals throughout the South in the USA, a statue of Albert Pike was toppled and set on fire in Washington DC on Juneteenth (19 June), the day that the end of slavery is celebrated in America. Pike was a prominent Freemason, and the only Confederate general with a statue in the US capital. He is also thought by many of his critics to have been a high-ranking member of the Ku Klux Klan.[55]

Condemnation by Trump and Johnson soon followed, with other politicians on both sides of the Atlantic quick to condemn the toppling of statues as mindless vandalism.

In the UK, far-right groups descended on the capital in the name of protecting statues and by extension white British history, leading to scenes of violence.[56]

The simple fact is that statues of slave traders belong in museums, not as monuments in our towns and cities, but we need to be careful that we don't lose sight of the deeper, more profound issues at stake. British historian David Olusoga wrote:

> *We do need to rethink who is memorialized in our public spaces. Bristol is a better city without Edward Colston. But statues are a symptom of the problem, not the problem itself. The real conversation has to be about racism and how we confront it.*[57]

A wider discussion about history and how we educate ourselves about the past is therefore vital. We shouldn't aim to erase history or rewrite it retrospectively, but we do need to reinstate positive black history, and acknowledge and include negative white history, such as colonialism. It is only by learning from the past that we can hope to avoid making the same mistakes again.

Education can play a key role here by ensuring an inclusive curriculum. Aside from the introduction of Black History Month (BHM) in schools, the negative impact of empire, for example, has been largely missing from everyday lessons, along with the achievements and contributions of black people, before, during and after slavery. Black people 'authored operas, pioneered secret algebra, erected ornate walls, pyramids, colossi, bridges, roads', and have as deep, rich and complex a history as anyone else.[58]

But while BHM is a step in the right direction, it shouldn't be necessary to devote time apart for black history; instead, it should be integral, so that a full spectrum of experiences is taught. We have a long way to go. David Olusoga again:

> We start from such a low base as our education system has, for decades, rejected pleas and requests made by two generations of black British people for black history to be made a core part of the national curriculum. As a result it is a national blind spot, a gap in our collective knowledge that affects us all — black and white . . .
>
> [Students] are being taught a whitewashed, sanitized version of the British past. One in which their stories, those that make sense of who they are and how they and their families came to be here and how they came to be British, have been largely omitted.[59]

Having experienced the absence of British black history at first hand, and the subsequent sense of disenfranchisement that accompanies it, School of Oriental and African Studies graduate Lavinya Stennett set up The Black Curriculum in 2019, an organization that campaigns for the year-round inclusion of black history in UK schools. They have created a black curriculum for eight to sixteen year olds, 'provide industry-leading consultation, teacher training and certification for schools', and advocate for their cause. Central to their ethos is a desire to move beyond the compartmentalized, narrow scope of the teaching of black history as it currently stands:

> Black British history is not merely a theme for October, but started hundreds of years before Windrush and predates European colonial enslavement. Our work aims to address and overcome these limitations by seeking to provide a contextual, globalized history that roots the black British experience in histories of movement and migration – 365 days a year.[60]

White people can participate in this process in a number of ways. First, you can look to fill the gaps left by an incomplete teaching of black history from your own education – for example, the true cost of the British Empire. More importantly, you can lend your support to people such as Lavinya Stennett by spreading her message or by donating to The Black Curriculum cause. You can even lobby your representatives to remove from our towns and cities monuments to figures from the past who should not in the twenty-first century be venerated for their exploitation of people of colour. Instead they should be placed in situations where their actions can be explained and put in context ... as long as you remember that there are bigger battles than statues that need to be fought and won if we are to defeat systemic racism once and for all.

Action Six

Create a level playing field
for women of colour

As we have already seen, a large proportion of black people and people of colour have to contend with discrimination and exclusion beyond just the colour of their skin, and we cannot understate the detrimental role gender plays when it comes racism. It is vital that modern-day allies recognize the intersectionality of gender and race that women of colour have to face, particularly black women, and that people of privilege acknowledge and appreciate the full implications of this. They must strive to create an environment that does not work against any aspect of the female identity and ensure women of colour have the necessary support to take advantage of opportunities that will allow them to progress towards parity with men in earning capacity and progression rates.

Sadly, that is not the case as it currently stands. I again return to the fact that there is only one black women in the *Sunday Times* Rich List. The situation is no better in the USA, despite the fact that black women are one of the most entrepreneurial groups in the country.[61] This demonstrates that the support they need to make the next step into the business elite is not currently forthcoming, highlighting a wider problem across society more generally. Part of the reason for this is the lack of start-up investment in businesses created by women entrepreneurs:

Just 13 per cent of senior people on UK investment teams are women, and almost half of investment teams have no women at all. This contributes to a stark gender imbalance in the businesses that investors decide to fund, just one in five of which is founded by a woman.[62]

Women, but especially women of colour, need to be supported and empowered to reach their full potential. And it is not just a matter of equality – our economy would be much stronger if we weren't missing out on the contribution of huge swathes of society:

The UK is losing out on £250 billion of economic value every year because women face barriers to becoming successful entrepreneurs, according to an independent review.[63]

Oprah Winfrey is a perfect example of what can be achieved. In the early 1980s, after establishing herself as a successful talk-show host in Chicago, she saw herself solely as a TV presenter until she appointed a lawyer called Jeff Jacobs to be her agent. He advised her that she should own her own business and brand, and she subsequently set up Harper Inc., now Harpo Productions, Inc. She also took full ownership of her programme and rebranded it as *The Oprah Winfrey Show*, growing it and her company into the entertainment juggernaut that it is today, and acting as the springboard for her aptly named TV channel OWN (The Oprah Winfrey Network). But it wouldn't have been possible if she had not been encouraged to look beyond the perceived limitations of her position: 'I had to get rid of that slave mentality. That's where Jeff came in. He took the ceiling off my brain'.[64] Winfrey is now the richest figure in entertainment and the first black woman billionaire in the world, providing a role model for women of colour in business to aspire to.

Investors need to look beyond the traditional groups, mainly consisting of white men, for the next generations of entrepreneurs, and business leaders must proactively seek out and create a level playing field for women of colour. Even the novice investor knows that the best way to achieve a return on your investment is to diversify your portfolio. If you invest all your capital in one place, you leave yourself vulnerable to fluctuations in that particular market. In the same way, companies need to ensure a diverse mix in their employee portfolio so that new ideas from people with different skills give them a competitive edge. Because when everybody thinks the same, we miss out on the opportunity to meet challenges with fresh ideas, we become complacent and we continue to do what we've always done before. The question that every company and every community has to ask is: 'Is everyone in the room?' It is also vital that more women of colour are hired to work in investment teams, allowing them to find diverse companies to invest in and potential untapped markets. How many more Oprah Winfreys might there be out there if only we removed the barriers to their success?

Action Seven

Make a bigger pie

One of the main aims of this book is to help people challenge their preconceptions and biases about race, unconscious or otherwise, and open themselves up to becoming allies to people of colour. It is not, by any means, about privileged white-bashing, but rather the opposite. My argument is that by operating in a more inclusive way towards *everyone* we will be able to realize the talents and potential of *everyone*. Scapegoating any one group or defining an individual solely by their otherness blocks us from having the honest and open dialogue we need in order to create a fairer society. To achieve a new 'business as unusual', we have to make a compelling case that demonstrates that diversity, and the dismantling of systemic racism, is better for everyone, even those who will need to share a little more than they have previously.

A major barrier to us creating more for everyone is income inequality. On one level, people of colour are more likely to occupy lower socioeconomic groups, thereby limiting their life chances – this is systemic racism in action. But many white working-class people also face extreme hardship, and unless we can address their concerns about globalization and immigration by providing ways for them to succeed too, it will make it much harder for us to address other areas of inequality. That is why a fairer system for all is the ultimate goal, rather than a situation whereby there are winners and losers.

We therefore need to think bigger and look for ways to increase the size of the pie so that there are enough slices for everyone. A more benevolent form of capitalism is required, one that does not seek to monopolize and eliminate competition but that shares innovation and develops a trampoline (as opposed to a safety net) that allows those who have fallen to jump up.

We have never in history experienced a situation whereby everyone was empowered to succeed to their full in this way, which means there is a huge pool of untapped potential out there. We are missing out on contributions that could make a difference, and each of us can take small actions to ensure we seek and value the widest range of people in order to redress the balance. Implement different ways to find talent, and search for it in new places. Also, in the workplace, think about who in your team might have been overlooked, despite their abilities – if you can see the people around you with fresh eyes, they can start to be rewarded on the basis of merit. Besides the moral imperative to pursuing this kind of equality, there is also a pragmatic reason. It is dangerous to exclude 'others', as there is a tipping point at which people will say enough is enough – inclusivity therefore promotes stability.

In Britain, on 14 June 2017, the stark effects of exactly this kind of growing income divide would test us to our limits when unimaginable tragedy struck. In the Royal Borough of Kensington and Chelsea, where the rich and poor live cheek by jowl, Grenfell Tower, a twenty-four-storey government block of 120 flats, housing 600 people, went up in flames, killing dozens of family members, neighbours and friends. What made it worse was that this disaster was preventable. The voracity of the fire was apparently exacerbated by flammable 'cosmetic' cladding from a £10-million facelift that was carried out the previous year.[65]

The inequality that led to a disaster such as Grenfell has to be addressed, especially as globalization and the changing demography of neighbourhoods will continue to be potential sources of tension. If we are not careful, communities under pressure, who feel that they are experiencing establishment neglect, will lash out in civil unrest, which will cost us all. In fact, we've already seen this happen again and again. In 2011, for example, riots broke out in the historically working-class neighbourhood of Tottenham, and then in other boroughs across London and other UK cities, in response to the police shooting of Mark Duggan, an unarmed black man.

To avoid scenes like those, and tragedies such as Grenfell, rather than ignore the plight and anger of people who feel disenfranchised and marginalized, it would be far more prudent for governments to invest in policies that include the talents of everyone, leading to a fairer society for all. It is people in positions of power who have to lead on this issue, so voting for political representatives who want to address inequality and systemic racism is key. As Atlanta-born rapper Killer Mike put it in his passionate speech in the wake of George Floyd's murder, the best course of action is 'to plot, plan, strategize, organize and mobilize' in order to hold our politicians to account.[66] Find out the candidates who have prioritized issues around race and diversity and lend them your support, either at the ballot box or by amplifying their message. Another less direct action would be to campaign for fairer voting systems and the enfranchisement of all people. This is a huge problem in the USA, where voter suppression is a key concern of people who want to tackle race inequality. Encouraging as many people as possible, but especially those from BAME and lower socioeconomic groups, to register to vote is therefore seen as an important way of tackling racism. The NBA superstar LeBron James, for example, has set up the non-profit organization More Than a Vote, 'advocating for NBA arenas and other large sports venues to be turned into mega polling sites' in advance of the presidential election in November 2020.[67] If everyone can vote, and every vote counts, we will make a great stride towards a more inclusive and fairer society. And it is only then that we will be able to create a big enough pie to feed everyone.

Action Eight

Be an ally, inspire more allies

Becoming a better ally in your own life, and taking personal action to be actively antiracist, is the first step in creating a fairer society, and an extremely important one. If people of privilege don't take individual responsibility for bringing about change, it won't be possible at all. But individual action is not enough. Instead, you must raise your standard and call your compatriots to follow you into the fray. In this way, the circle of influence can be expanded, and real momentum can be achieved.

It is easy to think that the best way to be successful in the fight against systemic racism is to seek out people who are overtly racist in order to challenge them and, in the process, bring them round to your way of thinking. But the truth is, it may be more effective to reach out to the people you know who are ambivalent about the problem, or who don't think it affects them, and bring them along with you. If you can arm allies with the right tools and inform people in your own groups, the message can spread far and wide, and the people with entrenched views increasingly become the marginalized minority.

That is not to say that we cannot and should not call out everyday racism in a positive and constructive way. The majority of us probably do not behave in an overtly racist way on an individual level and know better than to employ prejudiced language. At the same time, most of us have almost certainly encountered this everyday racism at some point in our lives. I bet most people reading this book have heard an elderly relative say something that made them feel uncomfortable, whether simply by using words that have become outdated or by expressing more explicitly racist views. It is easy to let this sort of thing pass, dismissing it as just a product of the person's upbringing – we often say things like, 'They did things differently in their generation'. However, I feel it is incumbent on all of us to challenge these views whenever we hear them, even if it is a loved one who is expressing them. But what is the best way to go about this without creating conflict and shame, which makes people defensive and closes down the conversation before a meaningful exchange can take place?

First, it is important to understand the context in which those views were formed. Although saying someone is from a different generation can be used to deflect from personal responsibility, there is also some truth in it. Our more elderly relatives were brought up in a time when there was less education about what constituted racist language and behaviour, so they often don't realize that their views could be wounding, and many would be mortified if they knew. At the same time, it's not a blame game but a reality check. Use the knowledge you have accumulated to help explain why their views are inaccurate, harmful, or both. One way to achieve this is to remind people of everyone's shared humanity – emotions, feelings and the importance of relationships are universal. Make appeals to people's own experiences of discrimination outside of racism – find the examples that resonate with them, and by doing so you may find that you are met with a positive response.

Even in extreme cases, people can be receptive to changing their points of view, and to breaking out of their respective bubbles to find some civil common ground, despite their wildly opposing opinions. In her TED talk, Megan Phelps-Roper, who left the infamous Westboro Baptist Church in Kansas after having been brought up as a member, describes how she and her husband met on social media, passionately disagreeing on a range of subjects but still becoming close friends.[68] She also offers some tips on how to talk and, more importantly, how to listen to people you don't agree with:

- Don't assume bad intent
- Ask questions – this helps us map the disconnect between different points of view and signals they are being heard
- Stay calm – it's OK to pause and revisit a contentious subject

- Make the argument but don't assume that your point of view is valid just because it's the point of view that you hold

These tips are certainly useful when it comes to our personal relationships, but they can also be helpful in the workplace and in the wider political sphere. And if progress is to be made, we need to avoid the echo chamber that comes with interacting only with those who share our own views.

At the same time, we cannot change everyone, so do not waste time trying to bring people around who have entrenched views that they are unwilling to examine – instead focus on those who are open to change and better understanding of other people's experiences. By creating more allies, by reaching out across the divide and by helping loved ones to understand the error of their ways, you can ensure that your effort to channel your privilege for good reaches the widest possible audience.

Action Nine

Redefine what it means to win

The economic sphere is one of the main arenas in which we see systemic inequality, so it is not going to be possible to move forward without a collective psychological shift in what it means to win. Wealth is currently the only measurement of success, but moral dimensions are just as important. Inclusion needs to be valued equally alongside wealth and profit as a measure of success, and people in positions of power need to redefine the terms of that success so inclusion is baked in – victory should only be possible if it is an inclusive, sustainable victory.

If you are in leadership, or in any role that measures and allocates rewards for success, then this call is directly to you to ensure that for a victory to be legitimate it must be inclusive. For example, targets that are linked to bonuses should be set with inclusion as a key criteria. This approach may well be unpopular initially, until the new culture has been embraced. And, in the short term,

it could result in a loss of business or inv
firms who have not been able to demon
inclusivity, but it will be transformative in t
to long term.

One example of a company that has decide
what success looks like is Metro Bank in the
Established in 2010, it was the first new high-street bank
in Britain for 100 years, and it has now grown to employ
almost 3,000 staff, with seventy stores across the country.
Although it has experienced ups and downs, it has defi-
nitely achieved success through its unique focus on its
people and innovative, inclusive processes. It invests in a
work culture that centres on diversity and people over
profit. One way it does this is by providing training to
recruitment managers, who are required to have a licence
to hire and must attend unconscious-bias and diversity
training programmes. The fruits of this effort are demonstrated by the fact that as of December 2019, 46 per cent
of the bank's workforce were from BAME backgrounds.[69]
This commitment to a different type of success is not,
however, at the expense of profit. As Danny Harmer, their
ex-Chief People Officer, put it:

> *Changing culture is more difficult than building a culture,*
> *and some banks don't have the alignment quite right*
> *between the measure of profit and sales, and managing*
> *people. As a result, people get left behind. But if you*
> *maintain your culture, offer customers choice and treat*
> *your staff well from the outset, you will be profitable.*[70]

er way to achieve inclusive success is to work with ocates for marginalized groups to come up with standards that really challenge the prevailing culture, creating a race to the top – an upwards race that leaves exclusive practices and attitudes behind. We have seen examples of this with the 'Top 100' lists of the best companies to work for with regards to areas such as gender, and in quality marks such as 'Confident on Disability' and Stonewall's LGBT awards.

While headway has been made when it comes to disability and LGBTQ+ equality in recent years, there are depressingly few examples of leaders or businesses who are putting this ethos into practice when it comes to race, highlighting the depth of the problem. This is perhaps due to the fact that race is the topic of inclusivity that people find most uncomfortable to confront. White people have the luxury of ignorance, as you don't experience racism at first hand – you can therefore try to avoid it or turn a blind eye, as long as you don't consider yourself to be racist on an individual level. But deep down most white people recognize their complicity, unintentionally or otherwise, in a system that has racism at its foundations. Jane Elliott, the anti-racism activist and educator, illustrated this point very clearly when she asked a room full of white people to stand up if they would be happy to be treated the way that black people are in the USA. When no one stood up, she revealed the implicit admission that this exposed – white people recognize black people are treated unfairly and would not wish that treatment for themselves.[71]

This was another reason why the murder of George Floyd was so impactful – white people have always known that this is the kind of danger that black people face, but it was now impossible to ignore. I don't, however, say any of this as a means of apportioning blame. Guilt blocks action, so we need to move away from this. We can't be paralyzed by fear and must instead contribute to changing things for the better. Only in this way will we be able to redefine what it means to win, for the benefit of everyone.

Action Ten

Act now

One of the main things I want you to take away from this book is that privilege can be a force for good – but only if you are willing to act. If you can focus on a real area of need alongside an area of strength, you will be able to initiate significant change.

In his bestselling book *Drive*, author Daniel Pink writes about the sage advice congresswoman Clare Boothe Luce gave to President John F. Kennedy in 1962:

'A great man,' she told him, 'is one sentence'. Franklin Roosevelt's was: 'He lifted us out of a great depression and helped us win a world war'. Luce feared that Kennedy's attention was so splintered among different priorities that his sentence risked becoming a muddled paragraph.[72]

Boothe Luce's words are as powerful today as they were when they were first uttered almost sixty years ago. They succinctly convey the point that to be effective you must be targeted and realistic in your approach. The truth is, most people will not be able to put into practice all of the tips I have given on how to be an ally to people of colour. Instead, you have to focus your attention where it can have the most impact.

In *Better Allies: Everyday Actions to Create Inclusive, Engaging Workplaces*, Karen Catlin, an American tech executive and advocate for inclusive workplaces, writes about the seven ways you can be an ally. These are:

1. The Sponsor – speak up in support in order to add credibility to and boost the standing and reputation of someone from an under-represented group (URG)
2. The Champion – willingly defer to people from URGs in more visible settings, creating opportunities for them to participate in meaningful ways
3. The Amplifier – create positive channels of communication and give a voice to people from URGs to ensure that they are heard
4. The Advocate – bring people from URGs into exclusive circles of influence and call out omissions when they occur
5. The Scholar – educate yourself about the challenges and prejudices faced by people from URGs. It is important to simply listen and learn;

this is not an opportunity for you to offer your own experiences and ideas. And you must do the work yourself, rather than waiting or expecting to be taught

6. The Upstander – see wrongdoing and act to confront it, and by doing so you will be the opposite of a bystander

7. The Confidant – create a safe space to allow people from URGs to express their fears, frustrations and needs – by listening and believing you go a long way to validating their experiences[73]

While these are focused on the workplace, they are all applicable more widely in our everyday lives – you may also recognize how they intersect with the ten actions I have described to channel your privilege. But it might not be possible to be all seven types of ally, at least not simultaneously. Choose when and how to adopt these positions in order to have the most impact. My team and I at the BBC Creative Diversity Unit have also created 'The Ally Track', a free tool that anyone who wants to be an ally can use to support this process.[74]

In addition to being targeted, the things you do must also have substance; it is not sufficient to enact performative allyship, which promotes statements of support over real action. As the protests in support of the Black Lives Matter movement gathered strength in June 2020, writer and editor Mireille Cassandra Harper posted on Twitter a list of ten things white people can do to move beyond performative, or optical, allyship, summarizing some of the advice offered by writers such as Layla Saad and Ibram X. Kendi. This list was then reproduced in full in *Vogue*:

1. Understand what optical allyship is
2. Check in on your black friends, family, partners, loved ones and colleagues
3. Be prepared to do the work
4. Read up on antiracist works
5. Avoid sharing content which is traumatic
6. Donate to funds and support initiatives
7. Do not centre this narrative around yourself
8. Keep supporting after the outrage
9. Stop supporting organizations that promote hate
10. Start your long-term strategy[75]

If you can put into practice even some of these points, or if you can adopt some of my suggestions, you can help to dismantle systemic racism, block by block. As we have seen, there are many ways you can use the power of privilege for good: be open to change, achieve awareness and move away from denial; do the little things, as even they can have a big impact, but do not wait for someone to ask you to participate; create sustainable diversity through ethical investment and informed consumerism; be courageous, dare to stand out from the crowd, and be willing to make difficult and unpopular decisions; educate yourself about the past and realize that there is more to history than the established, mainstream narratives include; be especially mindful of the intersection of race and gender; help to create a bigger pie so there is enough for everyone – inclusion is not about redefining who the winners and losers are, but instead creating an environment in which everyone can be a winner in the best way possible for them; expand the circle of influence by engaging more allies, reaching out across the divide and helping to educate ill-informed loved ones; and help to redefine the terms of success, with inclusion and equality baked in.

We can really do it – we all have the power and opportunity to write a new script and be part of something new and meaningful. But it is white people of privilege in particular who must be willing to make a real difference – up until now they have not been actively involved in sizeable enough numbers in the effort to challenge systemic racism. Think about what you want your life sentence to be, particularly in terms of your legacy when it comes to combatting racism. Real action can lead to real change – for everyone.

BE THE CHANGE

I refuse to allow any man-made differences to separate me from any other human beings.

Maya Angelou

We all seek to better ourselves and our environment, but we often struggle to know how to achieve this. Invariably, the answer that comes back to us time and again is that we, as Gandhi said, must 'Be the change that you wish to see in the world'.

If doing just that and taking the 'other way' takes a lifetime, it would at least be a lifetime well spent. And even if, like Martin Luther King, we don't get to see the promised land for ourselves, we would at least be able to see the incremental benefits of the 'other way', as every single positive intervention, no matter how small, will have an outcome that will perpetuate, just as every single neglect and exclusion, no matter how small, has regressive results with lasting consequences. And we would be able to exit this world with the knowledge that we were leaving it a better place than we found it. King may not have seen that brave new world that he dreamt of, but he knew what it would look like:

When this happens . . . we will be able to speed up that day when all of God's children, black men and white men, Jews and Gentiles, Protestants and Catholics, will be able to join hands and sing in the words of the old Negro spiritual: Free at last! Free at last!

This sounds to me like a pretty great place in which to live. And we can make this a reality. We can redesign society so that people from all backgrounds are able to contribute, and we can all work together towards building a society where equality, diversity and inclusion form the very heart of progress and eventually become the 'new normal'. We all have our part to play. It's time to figure out what our role is in shaping a better future – it may be how we hire, how we create policy, how we campaign, or how we love.

What it will be for all of us is how we think. How we think is what will create the future we all wish to see. We have to believe it, act upon it and then we can live it. It's easy to be cynical, but like Martin Luther King Jr we must all be dreamers in order to take a fairer future from a dream to reality. If we all endeavour to diversify our lives and act to challenge racism, the 'other' will cease to exist and we will no longer define ourselves by what separates us, but rather by what unites us as human beings, just trying to make the most of the short time we have on this planet we all call home. A fairer future is possible and can be achieved – we all just need to play our part.

SELECTED FURTHER READING AND RESOURCES

Books

Akala *Natives: Race and Class in the Ruins of Empire*

Bhopal, Kalwant *White Privilege: The Myth of a Post-racial Society*

Brathwaite, Candice *I Am Not Your Baby Mother: What It's Like to Be a Black British Mother*

Catlin, Karen *Better Allies: Everyday Actions to Create Inclusive, Engaging Workplaces*

Coates, Ta-Nehisi *Between the World and Me*

Diop, Cheikh Anta *Precolonial Black Africa: A Comparative Study of the Political and Social Systems of Europe and Black Africa, from Antiquity to the Formation of Modern States*

Diop, Cheikh Anta *The African Origin of Civilization: Myth or Reality?*

Eddo-Lodge, Reni *Why I'm No Longer Talking to White People About Race*

Hirsch, Afua *Brit(ish): On Race, Identity and Belonging*

Jablonski, Nina *Living Color: The Biological and Social Meaning of Skin Color*

Johnson, Allan G. *What Is a System of Privilege?*

Johnson, Allan G. *Privilege, Power and Difference*

Kendall, Mikki *Hood Feminism: Notes from the Women White Feminists Forgot*

Kendi, Ibram X. *How to Be an Antiracist*

Malik, Nesrine *We Need New Stories: Challenging the Toxic Myths Behind Our Age of Discontent*

Morrison, Toni *Mouth Full of Blood: Essays, Speeches, Meditations*

Obama, Barack *Dreams from My Father: A Story of Race and Inheritance*

Obama, Michelle, *Becoming*

Oluo, Ijeoma *So You Want to Talk About Race*

Olusoga, David *Black and British: A Forgotten History*

Rutherford, Adam *How to Argue With a Racist: History, Science, Race and Reality*

Saad, Layla *Me and White Supremacy: How to Recognise Your Privilege, Combat Racism and Change the World*

Shukla, Nikesh *The Good Immigrant*

Stevenson, Bryan *Just Mercy: A Story of Justice and Redemption*

Walker, Robin *Black History Matters*

Ward, Jesmyn *The Fire This Time: A New Generation Speaks About Race*

Wells, Spencer *The Journey of Man: A Genetic Odyssey*

Williams, Sophie *Anti-Racist Ally: An Introduction to Action and Activism*

Websites

www.blackhistorymonth.org.uk

www.blacklivesmatter.com

www.diversify.org

www.guidetoallyship.com

www.janeelliott.com

www.theblackcurriculum.com

REFERENCES

1 https://nationalseedproject.org/Key-SEED-Texts/white-privilege-unpacking-the-invisible-knapsack

2 https://www.agjohnson.us/glad/what-is-a-system-of-privilege/

3 https://fortune.com/2017/06/09/white-men-senior-executives-fortune-500-companies-diversity-data/

4 https://www.cnbc.com/2019/11/13/britains-top-100-companies-have-just-6-female-ceos-study-finds.html

5 https://www.theguardian.com/us-news/2020/may/26/george-floyd-killing-police-video-fbi-investigation

6 https://edition.cnn.com/2020/05/26/us/central-park-video-dog-video-african-american-trnd/index.html

7 https://www.thetimes.co.uk/article/why-is-valerie-moran-the-only-black-woman-on-the-sunday-times-rich-list-asks-june-sarpong-0h6nqpbc9

8 *Requiem for the American Dream* by Noam Chomsky, Seven Stories Press, 2017

9 https://www.oxfam.org/en/press-releases/just-8-men-own-same-wealth-half-world

10 *The Precariat: The New Dangerous Class*, Glasgow Centre for Population Health, Guy Standing Seminar, 22 November 2011

11 https://hbr.org/2016/11/why-diverse-teams-are-smarter

12 https://www.bbc.co.uk/news/uk-52219070

13 https://www.bbc.co.uk/news/world-us-canada-52905408

14 http://www.ucpress.edu/book.php?isbn=9780520283862

15 'Why racism doesn't go away' by Nina Jablonski for the *DNA Summit* magazine

16 'Why racism doesn't go away' by Nina Jablonski for the *DNA Summit* magazine

17 *The Journey of Man: A Genetic Odyssey* by Spencer Wells (Penguin, 2003)

18 http://ngm.nationalgeographic.com/2006/03/human-journey/shreeve-text/2

19 https://www.independent.co.uk/news/science/spencer-wells-at-root-were-still-hunters-1993055.html

20 Report of The Sentencing Project to the United Nations Human Rights Committee: Regarding Racial Disparities in the United States Criminal Justice. Published August 2013

21 According to the report, *Unlocking America: Why and How to Reduce America's Prison Population*: http://www.jfa-associates.com/publications/srs/UnlockingAmerica.pdf

22 https://www.theguardian.com/uk-news/2020/apr/23/knife-offences-hit-record-high-in-2019-in-england-and-wales

23 http://www.law.umich.edu/special/exoneration/Pages/about.aspx

24 www.nytimes.com/2017/03/07/us/wrongful-convictions-race-exoneration.html?mcubz=3

25 *Just Mercy* by Bryan Stevenson (Random House, 2015)

26 Bureau of Justice Assistance – US Department of Justice, Research Summary: Plea and Charge Bargaining

27 https://time.com/4716111/maxine-waters-bill-oreilly-fox/

28 http://www.bbc.co.uk/news/world-us-canada-38301808

29 http://www.news.com.au/sport/tennis/venus-williams-called-gorilla-in-espns-australian-open-commentary/news-story/1b70be84a4fd3c820ecc67ae5f0f7cf9

30 https://www.nytimes.com/2014/09/21/arts/television/viola-davis-plays-shonda-rhimess-latest-tough-heroine.html?_r=1

31 https://www.thesun.co.uk/tvandshowbiz/3283150/freida-pinto-cries-sky-drama-guerrilla

32 www.theguardian.com/media/2020/aug/24/david-olusoga-his-edinburgh-television-festival-speech-in-full

33 Oprah Winfrey CBS Special with Michelle Obama, 27 December 2016

34 http://www.bbc.co.uk/news/magazine-37799305

35 *Living Color: The Biological and Social Meaning of Skin Color* Nina Jablonski (University of California Press, 2012)

36 'Race at The Top' 2014 – study by Race for Opportunity, part of the (BITC) Business in the Community: http://race.bitc.org.uk/all-resources/research-articles/race-top

37 ibid.

38 https://www.amnesty.org.uk/press-releases/brendan-cox-calls-britains-communities-fight-alarming-rise-populism

39 http://www.independent.co.uk/news/uk/home-news/finsbury-park-attack-far- right-extremist-rise-year-statistics-prevent-terrorism-scheme-referrals-a7798231.html

40 https://www.bbc.co.uk/news/world-us-canada-48806265

41 https://www.youtube.com/watch?v=3g_zSvtSs-A

42 https://www.fnlondon.com/articles/the-23-year-old-whose-finance-career-started-with-knocking-on-kensington-doors-20190121

43 https://www.vercida.com/uk/articles/reggie-nelson

44 https://www.nfl.com/news/colin-kaepernick-explains-why-he-sat-during-national-anthem-0ap3000000691077

45 https://www.chicagotribune.com/sports/ct-nfl-has-blackballed-colin-kaepernick-20170323-story.html

46 https://www.politico.com/story/2017/09/22/trump-nfl-protests-football-243046

47 https://www.cbsnews.com/news/colin-kaepernick-nike-6-billion-man/

48 https://www.census.gov/quickfacts/fact/table/US/PST045219

49 https://purpose.nike.com/fy19-representation-and-pay

50 https://www.bbc.co.uk/mediacentre/latestnews/2020/creative-diversity-commitment

51 https://theundefeated.com/features/why-did-black-lives-matter-protests-attract-unprecedented-white-support/

52 https://www.goodreads.com/quotes/9150190-if-you-can-convince-the-lowest-white-man-he-s-better

53 https://www.bbc.co.uk/news/uk-47300343

54 https://deadline.com/2020/06/bame-tv-workers-write-to-major-uk-networks-government-demanding-change-1202963792/

55 https://www.theguardian.com/us-news/2020/jun/20/protesters-statue-washington-dc-albert-pike-juneteenth-us

56 https://www.standard.co.uk/news/uk/right-wing-protesters-parliament-square-statues-a4468171.html

57 https://www.theguardian.com/global/2020/jun/14/statue-wars-must-not-distract-reckoning-with-racism-david-olusoga

58 *Between the World and Me* by Ta-Nehisi Coates (The Text Publishing Company, 2015)

59 https://www.theguardian.com/books/2020/jun/15/britain-can-no-longer-ignore-its-darkest-chapters-we-must-teach-black-history

60 https://www.theblackcurriculum.com/

61 https://www.forbes.com/sites/nextavenue/2018/09/09/black-women-entrepreneurs-the-good-and-not-so-good-news/#20046efc6ffe

62 https://www.independent.co.uk/news/business/analysis-and-features/uk-startups-gender-bias-women-entrepreneurs-virgin-a9064806.html

63 ibid.

64 https://www.forbes.com/sites/jennifereum/2014/09/29/how-oprah-went-from-talk-show-host-to-first-african-american-woman-billionaire/#51c0bd006163

65 https://www.insidehousing.co.uk/news/news/grenfell-inquiry-acm-cladding-was-primary-cause-of-fire-spread-and-tower-did-not-comply-with-regulations-judge-rules-63929

66 https://www.bbc.co.uk/news/av/world-us-canada-52860643/george-floyd-death-rapper-killer-mike-s-plea-to-protesters-in-atlanta

67 https://bleacherreport.com/articles/2898497-lebron-james-more-than-a-vote-pushing-nba-arenas-as-mega-polling-sites

68 https://www.youtube.com/watch?v=bVV2Zk88beY

69 https://www.metrobankonline.co.uk/about-us/culture-diversity/

71 http://www.diversify.org/metro-bank-case-study.html

72 https://www.youtube.com/watch?v=4yrg7vV4a5o

73 *Drive: The Surprising Truth about What Motivates Us* by Daniel Pink (Canongate Books, 2018)

74 https://www.themuse.com/advice/what-is-an-ally-7-examples

75 https://www.bbc.co.uk/creativediversity/

76 https://www.vogue.co.uk/arts-and-lifestyle/article/non-optical-ally-guide

ACKNOWLEDGEMENTS

To all my allies, old and new, there are far too many to mention. I'm incredibly grateful to you all, but special thanks go to the following people for being true agents for change!

Lucy Bayliss
Sarah Baynes
Sara Brown
Matt Browne
Simon Collins
Dr Frances Corner
Sue Cowhig
Tim Davie
David de Rothschild
Victoria Finch
Mark Florman
Miriam González Durántez
Tony Hall
Graham Hill
Vernon Kay

Baroness Margaret
    McDonagh
Caroline Michel
Lisa Milton
Charlotte Moore
Greg Nugent
Dermot O'Leary
Jim O'Neill
Jimmy O'Reilly (RIP)
Charlie Redmayne
Roland Rudd
Caroline Rush
Bob Shennan
Richard Thompson
Shelley Zallis

Could inclusivity
be the key to success?

In *Diversify,* June Sarpong OBE puts the spotlight on groups who are often marginalized in our society – including women, those living with disabilities, and the LGBTQ+ community.

With evidence from Oxford University, she proves how a more open approach to how we work, learn, and live will help us reach our maximum potential, lessen the pressure on the state, and solve some of the most stubborn challenges we face.

**_Diversify_ by June Sarpong –
available in print, eBook and audio now.**

'A handbook for these troubled times'
Psychologies

'Engaging and informative . . . highlights our common humanity' Kofi Annan

#Diversify

Printed in Great Britain
by Amazon